Wake Up and Smell the Coffee -

Pacific Northwest Edition

Laura Zahn

Down to Earth Publications
St. Paul, Minnesota

Other recent or soon-to-be-published books by Laura Zahn:

Chocolate for Breakfast and Tea (ISBN 0-939301-97-0)
Innkeepers' Best Low-Fat Breakfasts (ISBN 0-939301-18-0)
Innkeepers' Best Muffins (ISBN 0-939301-96-2)
WAKE UP & SMELL THE COFFEE - Northern New England Edition (ISBN 0-939301-13-X)
WAKE UP & SMELL THE COFFEE - Southwest Edition (ISBN 0-939301-92-X)
WAKE UP & SMELL THE COFFEE - Lake States Edition (ISBN 0-939301-94-6)
Bringing Baby Home: An Owner's Manual for First-Time Parents (ISBN 0-939301-91-1)

To Dad,

Edward R. Zahn,

who was so much more

than EZ Finance

*'We don't want you eating
crackers and beans'*

Published by **Down to Earth Publications**
1032 West Montana Avenue
St. Paul, Minnesota 55117

ISBN 0-939301-10-5

Library of Congress Cataloging in Publication Data

Zahn, Laura C., 1957-
    Wake Up and Smell the Coffee - Lakes States Edition.

    Includes index.

1. Breakfasts   2. Cookery   3. Bed and Breakfast Accommodations - Pacific Northwest - Directories

TX 733.Z3

Dewey System - Ideas and Recipes for Breakfast and Brunch - 641.52

Cover Illustration by Lynn Fellman, Golden Valley, Minnesota

Maps by Jim Miller, St. Paul, Minnesota

Many thanks to
Kathy O'Neill, Ed Zahn, Mary Zahn,
Kristina Ford, Ann Burckhardt, Susan Hansen,
Lisa Watt, Wes Wilson, Jim and Chris Moore,
Wendy Maroun, Elaine Garner, Helen Hecker,
Marilyn, Tom and the Voyageur Press staff and sales reps,
Leslie Dimond, Lynn Fellman,
and my handsome husband, Jim Miller.

Special thanks to the innkeepers
for sharing their best recipes and artwork,
for their cooking hints and ideas,
for their contacts and willingness to "spread the word"
and for their enthusiasm and encouragement.

I also thank them for the privilege
of being the "middleperson" in communicating their favorite recipes
to many hungry cooks and readers.

Introduction

"Wake Up and Smell the Coffee." And the Sour Cream Coffeecake. And the Ginger Pear Muffins. And the 60 Minute Cinnamon Rolls.

Is your mouth watering yet? Alarm clocks or wake up knocks are often unnecessary at these Oregon and Washington B&Bs. The aroma of a breakfast bread, coffeecake, or even pancakes on the griddle or an egg dish in the oven easily wafts up the stairs, floats under doorways and nudges awake even the most sound sleepers.

Perhaps you remember staying at Grandma's house that way. Because "waking up and smelling the coffee" is such a special experience, only B&B inns small enough so that guests literally can smell breakfast cooking were invited to participate in this cookbook. No recipes were included from hotels or even guest cottages where baking and cooking is done in another house.

Lovers of small B&Bs will understand why this exclusivity makes a difference. If you haven't yet tried B&Bs, be careful — once you try staying in them, you may not be satisfied in another motel, hotel or rental cabin. Their brand of hospitality is, indeed, very different.

And that's why this is more than a cookbook. In order to get more of the "flavor" of the inn and innkeeper from whom the recipe came, information about the people and place is included below each recipe. If you're more than an armchair traveler, do try to visit the inns that sound appealing to you. Their addresses and phone numbers are listed so you can contact them directly for more information, and a map is included to give you an idea of their locations. All B&Bs in this book take reservations directly, without the need to go through a reservation service.

Every B&B is unique. That's their beauty. Likewise, every B&B breakfast is different. There are some common characteristics, however.

Wise innkeepers, for instance, know how important food is to "the B&B experience." (Indeed, any host knows guests feel more comfortable and welcome when offered food and drink.) A groaning board is not necessary, but plentiful, tasty food is. In this cookbook, you'll find recipes for everything from a simple fruit dish that is part of a continental breakfast to Plum Cheese Blintzes and Souffle Roll, rather time-consuming but spectacular entrees that are part of an elaborate, unforgettable breakfast.

Also universal — at least to the B&Bs in this cookbook — is an affinity for homemade, "from-scratch" cooking. There *is* a difference between from-scratch buttermilk pancakes and buttermilk pancakes from a box. (And the surprising thing, for those of us raised in the '50s or '60s on food that came from a box, is that the from-scratch ones aren't difficult at all.)

In this rushed, toaster pastry/breakfast bar/powdered breakfast milkshake world, when was the last time you ate a *real* breakfast? And plain old bacon-and-eggs don't count.

We are talking "slow foods" here. If you say, "I'm not much of a breakfast eater," I would respond that if you define "cold cereal" as "breakfast," than neither am I. But if we are talking about a *real* breakfast of, say, hot muffins, fresh fruit, and a flavorful egg casserole or homemade pancakes with warmed fruit sauce or maple syrup — well, who can say he or she is not an eater of that kind of breakfast?

It's ludicrous to think that many American families get up at the crack of dawn to bake and cook and start their day with such a repast. But more are taking extra time on weekends to dabble in the kitchen, to fix weekend brunches with friends, or to make homemade breakfast food, then reheating it weekday mornings. They, too, have found that the short-cut "pre-fab" foods may temporarily appease the body but do nothing to nourish the soul. "Comfort food," on the other hand, is satisfying for its nourishment and through its aroma, texture and taste. The act of cooking from-scratch itself can be deeply rewarding.

Relaxing at a small B&B, getting up a little later and having breakfast prepared for you and prettily served in a dining room is a big treat. The innkeeper might be up early with the yeast dough, or the innkeeper might be wrestling with a kitchen counter full of dirty dishes, but guests need not lift a finger. On *that* basis, I don't know anyone who "isn't a breakfast eater."

It's true that these recipes might be less romantic at home where no one else will scrub the muffin tins. But still, these recipes are an excellent start for those who want to return to (or discover) real breakfasts. No other meal has the comforting aromas of breakfast. Smells are carried more acutely and accurately in our memories than any of our other senses. It seems each of us carries around a scent storage file that's suddenly flung open to reveal a time and place we'd long since tucked away. Overnights at B&Bs with home-cooked breakfasts are sure to create new favorite aroma "files." So can these recipes in your own kitchen.

Many of the recipes included are simple and some can be made ahead of time. Most innkeepers encouraged creativity in adapting these recipes (in fact, they often devised them through experimentation themselves). As you read, you'll discover many recipes already have improved on great basic ideas (for instance, isn't Dessert for Breakfast long overdue?). And the food certainly is not limited to consumption only at breakfast or brunch — after all, "pancake suppers" are a fine idea. Don't miss the "Other Favorites," recipes that innkeepers serve as hors d'oeuvres, as side dishes or to stock the cookie jar. Innkeepers truly have shared their best recipes in this collection.

While compiling this cookbook, I saw my print-outs of favorite recipes become sprinkled and smeared with the kitchen "batter spatters" that show heavy use. I hope that, in time, your cookbook will display the same evidence of being well-used and well-loved.

Contents

Breads

Preserves, Butters, Spreads & Sauces

Fruits

Entrees

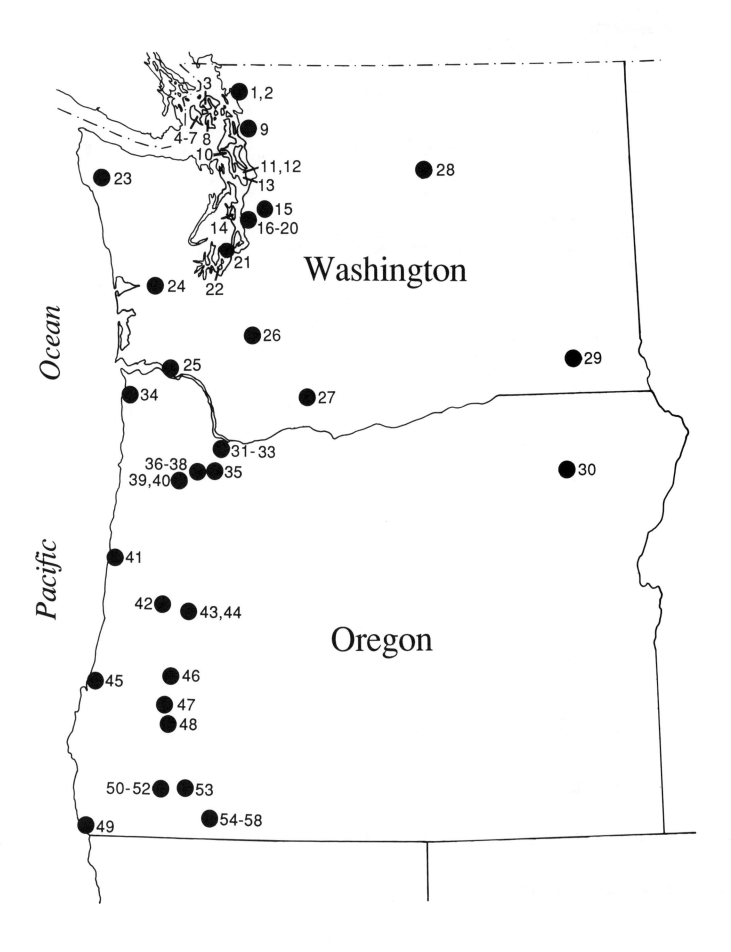

WASHINGTON

1. Bellingham - *DeCann House B&B*
2. Bellingham - *North Garden Inn*
3. Orcas Island - *Turtleback Farm Inn*
4. San Juan Island - *Blair House*
5. San Juan Island - *Moon and Sixpence Inn*
6. San Juan Island - *Olympic Lights*
7. San Juan Island - *Westwinds B&B*
8. Lopez Island - *The Inn at Swifts Bay*
9. Mount Vernon - *The White Swan Guest House*
10. Coupeville (Whidbey Island) - *The Victorian B&B*
11. Langley (Whidbey Island) - *Eagles Nest Inn*
12. Langley (Whidbey Island) - *Log Castle B&B*
13. Clinton (Whidbey Island) - *Home by the Sea*
14. Bainbridge Island - *The Bombay House B&B*
15. Redmond - *Cedarym*
16. Seattle - *Chambered Nautilus*
17. Seattle - *Chelsea Station*
18. Seattle - *Marit's B&B*
19. Seattle - *Mildred's B&B*
20. Seattle - *Salibury House*
21. Gig Harbor - *Tall Ship Ketch Krestine*
22. Anderson Island - *The Inn at Burg's Landing*
23. Forks - *Miller Tree Inn*
24. Montesano - *The Sylvan Haus*
25. Cathlamet - *The Gallery B&B at Little Cape Horn*
26. Morton - *St. Helens Manorhouse*
27. Trout Lake - *Mio Amore Pensione*
28. Pateros - *Amy's Manor B&B*
29. Dayton - *Syndicate Hill B&B*

OREGON

30. LaGrande - *Stange Manor B&B*
31. Portland - *The Clinkerbrick House*
32. Portland - *General Hooker's House*
33. Portland - *Portland Guest House*
34. Seaside - *The Gilbert Inn*
35. Wilsonville - *The Willows B&B*
36. Newberg - *Littlefield House*
37. Newberg - *The Smith House B&B*
38. Newberg - *Spring Creek Llama Ranch*
39. McMinnville - *Orchard View Inn*
40. McMinnville - *Steiger Haus*
41. Seal Rock - *The Blackberry Inn*
42. Elmira - *McGillivray's Log Home B&B*
43. Eugene - *Getty's Emerald Garden B&B*
44. Eugene - *Maryellen's Guest House*
45. North Bend - *Baywood-on-the-Water*
46. Oakland - *The Pringle House B&B*
47. Roseburg - *Umpqua House of Oregon*
48. Myrtle Creek - *Sonka's Sheep Station Inn*
49. Brookings - *The Ward House B&B*
50. Grants Pass - *Ahlf House B&B*
51. Grants Pass - *The Handmaiden's Inn*
52. Grants Pass - *Riverbanks Inn*
53. Gold Hill - *Willowbrook Inn*
54. Ashland - *The Cowslip's Belle*
55. Ashland - *Hersey House*
56. Ashland - *The Morical House*
57. Ashland - *Mt. Ashland Inn*
58. Ashland - *Romeo Inn*

Things You Should Know

> Before beginning, please read the entire recipe to find out how hot to preheat the oven, what size pan(s) to grease, or how many hours or days ahead of time the recipe must be started.

> Baking and cooking temperatures are listed in degrees Fahrenheit.

> Remember to preheat the oven to the temperature listed in the recipe before baking.

> Assume that white (granulated) sugar is called for in these recipes when the ingredients list "sugar." Powdered (confectioner's) or brown sugar are listed as such.

> Brown sugar is "packed" into the measuring cup, not loose, unless otherwise specified.

> When making yeast breads, read the yeast instructions thoroughly. For yeast breads or for preserves and recipes which involve canning, you may wish to consult a cookbook with detailed instructions for these processes.

> Recipes have been listed in chapters according to the way in which innkeepers serve them. For instance, you will find some fruit dishes in chapters other than "Fruits," and dishes that could be suitable as "Dessert for Breakfast" are included in other chapters because the innkeepers serve them as snacks, holiday fare or even entrees. The table of contents, therefore, also serves as an index so you can double-check other chapters at a glance.

> While the format of the recipes has been standardized, the directions remain in the words of the innkeepers as much as possible. Innkeepers had the opportunity to double-check their recipes before printing.

> Most innkeepers encouraged experimentation with their recipes, such as substituting or adding ingredients for personal preferences or health reasons. Many of these recipes, they said, were devised through their experimentation with a basic recipe.

Why start the morning with the same old (boring) glass of orange juice? B&Bs break all the rules for the morning eye-opener. Many B&Bs serve a variety of unusual juices, fresh-grind the coffee beans or stir a little almond-flavored liqueur into the morning coffee or peach schnapps into orange juice. Read on to see how some innkeepers provide more nourishment by adding fresh fruit in impressive "smoothie" blender drinks. And to welcome guests on a chilly evening, or to celebrate a special day, innkeepers concoct soothing hot beverages.

Beverages

Any Time Herbal Tea

Ingredients:

4 ounces each:
   fennel seed
   anise seed
   dill seed
   spearmint leaves, dried
   peppermint leaves, dried
2 ounces licorice root, dried

> Mix all ingredients well and keep in a canister.
> Put 1/3 cup tea to 2 quarts water in a stainless steel pot.
> Bring to boiling, simmer 2 minutes and let steep.
> Strain and serve.

1/3 cup tea makes 8-10 servings

from **The Ward House B&B**
516 Redwood Street
P.O. Box 86
Brookings, OR 97415
503-469-5557

This herb tea "was the house tea at our former restaurant and is now welcoming guests with its sweet aroma," said Innkeeper Gro Lent. She puts the tea in a serving pot on a hot plate so it's available anytime to guests.

In addition to its aromatic qualities, "this tea aids in digestion. I was trained in foot reflexology 10 years ago and this recipe came from my teacher, who was very knowledgeable in natural health."

Fascination with the B&B concept began in Norway for Gro (pronounced "Grew"), where she stayed in hostels similar to B&Bs while hiking around a mountain with high school friends.

Some of the herbs for this tea come from Gro's garden. She attended the California School of Herbal Studies in 1979 and studied foot reflexology the following year. "I believe in cultivating that which is natural," she said.

Other Ward House recipes:
Norwegian Waffles, page 123
Chocolate Sauerkraut Cake, page 145

Fruit Smoothie

Ingredients:
    2 ripe bananas, frozen for 24 hours or more
    1 cup frozen peaches, berries, melon or other fruit
    1 cup apple or other juice (coconut-pineapple is suggested)

> Ahead of time, peel very ripe bananas and seal in a freezer bag. These should be frozen for at least 24 hours.
> If possible, use fresh summer fruit for the second ingredient. Do not use apples or pears. Wrap and freeze as you did bananas. If no fresh fruit is available, use frozen, unsweetened fruit from the grocery store.
> Pour juice into the blender.
> Add frozen bananas. Blend at high speed until well-blended.
> Add other frozen fruit and blend again.
> If necessary, add a little more juice; the drink should be the consistency of a malt.
> Serve and consume immediately.

Makes 2 servings

from **Umpqua House of Oregon**
7338 Oak Hill Road
Roseburg, OR 97470
503-459-4700

Innkeeper Rhoda Mozorosky invented this recipe because "I did not want my husband to consume as many ice cream malts as he did!" It also satisfies her sweet tooth without adding many calories.

Rhoda and husband Allen opened their two-guestroom B&B in 1987 after remodeling this large home. They took early retirement from careers in Los Angeles to enter innkeeping in Oregon.

Rhoda may sit with guests, sipping this smoothie, while Allen fixes omelettes or waffles. From the dining area, guests have a view of Umpqua Valley and the 6.5 wooded acres on which the home sits. Many of the fruits, vegetables and eggs served come from Mozorosky's organic garden and chickens.

Other Umpqua House recipes:
Cranberry Crisp Coffeecake, page 27
Pumpkin Muffins, page 45
High Energy Fruit Balls, page 158

Homemade Hot Mulled Cider

Ingredients:

1 cup sugar
24 whole cloves
1 stick cinnamon
1/2 lemon, sliced
1/2 cup water
4 cups apple cider, fresh
2 cups pineapple juice
2 cups orange juice

> Combine the sugar, spices, lemon slices and water in a saucepan. Boil for 5 minutes.
> Remove from heat. Strain the liquid into a large pot. Discard the cloves, cinnamon stick and lemon slices.
> Add cider and juices. Heat through and serve.

Makes 6-8 servings

from **Hersey House**
451 North Main Street
Ashland, OR 97520
503-482-4563

Guests may be greeted in the late afternoon or after an Oregon Shakespeare Festival performance with a steaming cup of this cider, an embellishment of what Oregon orchards provide. It's also a welcome addition to holiday parties and fills the entire house with its aroma, said Innkeeper Gail Orell.

In 1983, Gail and her sister, Lynn Savage, returned to the hometown of their great-grandfather, who taught school in Ashland in the early 1890s. The sisters bought a 1904 modified salt box, and restored, redecorated and landscaped it. A year later, they opened the Hersey House.

Inside, the four guestrooms are decorated with coordinated wallcoverings and linens, each with antiques and a Victorian theme. Home to five generations of Herseys, Hersey family portraits decorate the walls. Outside, an English country garden has been added, from which come most of the inn's garnishes and herbs and fresh flowers for the rooms.

Other Hersey House recipes:
Strawberry French Toast, page 110
Gingerbread Pancakes, page 116
Plum Cheese Blintzes, page 127
Cranberry Sherbet, page 136

Hot Vanilla

Ingredients:

1 cup milk
1 teaspoon honey
1 drop pure vanilla extract
Tiny pinch of cinnamon

> Heat milk until very hot but not boiling.
> Pour into mug and add honey, vanilla and cinnamon. Stir and serve.

Makes 1 serving

from **Willowbrook Inn**
628 Foots Creek Road
Gold Hill, OR 97525
503-582-0075

"Our children preferred this to the more usual hot chocolate, and it's an old family Christmas morning favorite," said Innkeeper JoAnn Hoeber. "We now offer it to our guests as a treat after skiing the slopes of Mt. Ashland."

The only difference between this beverage and one made at other people's homes is that Hoebers use honey from their own bees, who "work" the flowers in their own English style herb garden. The gigantic garden features more than 100 varieties of herbs, which often go into the breakfasts for their B&B guests.

JoAnn and Tom moved into their Gold Hill home after owning and operating a kitchenware store in the San Francisco Bay area. The home was built in 1905 by a mining family which was successful in pursuit of gold. Located on 2.5 acres, Hoebers inn, opened in 1988, has two guestrooms. The acreage has room for chickens, goats and bees. Guests may see deer in the meadow while sitting on the porch or enjoy a bike ride through the rolling hills of southern Oregon.

The inn is located near the Rogue River, 30 minutes from Ashland and 20 minutes from the historic gold mining town of Jacksonville.

Other Willowbrook Inn recipes:
Herb Garden Frittata, page 99
Gold Nugget Cakes with Peach Sauce, page 117

Pina Colada Smoothies

<u>*Ingredients:*</u>
  1 banana
  1 cup crushed pineapple, undrained
  1 cup bottled pina colada daiquiri mix
  1 cup pina colada natural juice beverage (such as Kern's coconut-pineapple nectar)
  1 cup pina colada low-fat yogurt
  4-5 ice cubes

> Place banana, pineapple, daiquiri mix and juice in blender. Blend until smooth.
> Add yogurt and ice cubes. Blend again.
> Place mixture in freezer until ready to serve (no longer than 45 minutes or so).
> At serving time, blend again and pour into champagne flutes. "The aroma is wonderful."

Makes 8 half-cup servings

from **The Morical House**
668 North Main Street
Ashland, OR 97520
503-482-2254

"Pete is the 'smoothie' expert," says Innkeeper Pat Dahl of her husband, civil engineer, globe trotter and co-innkeeper. She credits him with experimenting and perfecting this recipe, which is served to guests either in the dining room — perhaps at Pat's grandmother's refinished oak dining room set — or on the sunporch, both of which overlook the Cascade Mountains.

Pat and Pete bought this existing inn in 1988, making a career switch to operate five guestrooms in a manner they say reflects "a less-frenzied era." They searched northern California and southern Oregon thoroughly before deciding on the Morical House, which originally opened in 1982. They felt at home in Ashland, with its unhurried atmosphere. Now they can retreat to their 1.5-acre yard, where deer and other wildlife occasionally visit to snack on some of the nearly 150 plant species in the gardens.

Dahls set other standards for their perfect B&B besides just liking the place. They insisted on finding a small, friendly community with major attractions and good restaurants — the same things that travelers like about Ashland.

Other Morical House recipes:
Celebration Eggs, page 90
Walnut Frosties, page 139

Cinnamon and breakfast go together like, well, like chocolate and nuts. And there's enough cinnamon in many of these tantalizing coffeecakes to fill the whole house with a comforting aroma and rouse anyone with half a sweet-tooth straight out of bed. The best thing about coffeecakes may be that it's socially acceptable to eat them for a first or main course rather than holding off until dessert. Many of these recipes showcase the Pacific Northwest's best fruits and nuts. They may taste like you slaved all day, but several recipes are fairly simple and quick to prepare.

Coffeecakes

Apple Bundt Cake

Ingredients:

3 cups flour
1/2 teaspoon salt
1 teaspoon baking soda
1 cup sugar
3 cups cooking apples, diced
1 cup nuts, chopped
2 eggs
3/4 cup vegetable oil
1 teaspoon vanilla extract

Topping:
1/4 cup butter, melted
2 tablespoons sugar
1 tablespoon light corn syrup
1 teaspoon vanilla extract

Also:

Powdered sugar

> In a large bowl, sift together flour, salt, soda and sugar.
> Stir in the apples and nuts.
> In a separate bowl, mix the eggs, oil and vanilla.
> Add egg mixture to flour mixture. Stir until well blended; mixture will resemble cookie dough.
> Pour into a greased and floured bundt (fluted tube) pan.
> Bake in a preheated oven at 350 degrees for 1 hour, 15 minutes.
> Meanwhile, blend all topping ingredients. After removing cake from oven, pour topping over the hot cake still in the pan, letting topping drizzle down the sides.
> Cool the cake for about 30 minutes. Remove from pan. Keep covered until time to serve. Dust with powdered sugar before serving.

Makes 12-18 servings

from **Mt. Ashland Inn**
550 Mt. Ashland Road
Ashland, OR 97520
503-482-8707

"I usually serve this with the fruit or juice course before the entree," said Innkeeper Elaine Shanafelt, who adapted a heavier version of this recipe until she perfected "the wonderful moist taste." As an added benefit, "it also fills the inn with wonderful aromas while baking."

Mt. Ashland Inn is a handcrafted cedar log home with five guestrooms located in the Siskiyou Mountains, 16 miles from Ashland with views of the Cascades and Mt. Shasta. Guests hike or cross-country ski from the door, and the Pacific Crest Trail passes through the inn's parking lot.

Another Mt. Ashland Inn recipe:
Baked Apples, page 77

Apple Morning Cake

Ingredients:

1-1/4 cups flour
1/2 cup sugar
1/2 teaspoon salt
1/2 teaspoon cinnamon
1/2 cup walnuts, chopped
2 tart green unpeeled apples, grated
1/2 cup milk
1 egg, beaten
3 tablespoons vegetable oil

Topping:
1/2 cup sour cream
1/2 cup sugar

> Mix flour, sugar, salt and cinnamon.
> Stir in walnuts and grated apples.
> In a separate bowl, mix milk, egg and oil.
> Add egg mixture to flour mixture, but be careful not to overmix.
> Pour into a greased 9-inch round cake pan.
> Mix sour cream and sugar topping. Drizzle over the top of the coffeecake.
> Bake in a preheated oven at 400 degrees for 30-35 minutes.

Makes 6 servings

from **Blair House**
345 Blair Avenue
Friday Harbor, WA 98250
206-378-5907

This coffecake is a favorite of Innkeepers Jane Benson and Jeff Zander, who bought this seven-guestroom inn in 1987. It's located in Friday Harbor on San Juan Island, about four blocks from the ferry landing.

Jane serves breakfast at a large dining room table near a fire in the woodstove in the fall and winter, or outside on the wrap-around porch or beside the heated swimming pool in the summer or spring. "I have always been interested in innkeeping since spending time in New England when I was going to college," she said. During a trip to the Pacific Northwest, she saw an ad for some live-in help at Blair House. "I thought it was the perfect opportunity to try the business before making an investment in it," she said. "One thing led to another, and we bought the business in December 1987." Jane has most of the innkeeping duties; Jeff is a marine engineer.

Another Blair House recipe:
Sour Cream Coffeecake, page 31

Applesauce Coffee Braid

Ingredients:

2 packages active dry yeast
1 cup warm water (not higher than 115 degrees)
1/2 cup butter, melted
1/2 cup sugar
4 eggs
1 teaspoon salt
5 cups flour
1-1/2 cups applesauce
1/4 cup milk

> In a large bowl, dissolve yeast in warm water.
> Add butter, sugar, 3 eggs and salt. Mix well. Then stir in flour.
> On a floured board, knead the dough until smooth.
> Put dough back in bowl, cover and refrigerate at least 4 hours.
> Cut dough into thirds. Roll out each third to an 8 x 12-inch rectangle.
> Spoon applesauce down the length of each rectangle.
> Fold dough over the filling to seal in applesauce. Repeat steps twice with rest of dough.
> Braid the three strips together. Place the braided roll on a greased cookie sheet.
> Cover with a towel and let rise 60-90 minutes or until doubled in size.
> Mix remaining egg with milk. Brush mixture over the top of braid.
> Bake in a preheated oven at 375 degrees for 25-35 minutes or until lightly browned and braid sounds hollow when tapped.

Makes 18-20 servings

from **The Inn at Burg's Landing**
8808 Villa Beach Road
Anderson Island, WA 98303
206-884-9185

Cinnamon, walnuts and raisins or chopped dates, or pureed pears, plums or peaches also make good fillings for this coffeecake, said Innkeeper Annie Burg. Annie uses homemade applesauce made with apples from their trees.

Guests can see this log inn when they arrive on the ferry from Steilacoom. The home has picture windows from which ferries and sailboats can be seen, and the windows open directly on Mt. Rainier. Two guestrooms, one on the main floor and one in the "loft," are available. Ken and Annie opened their home as a B&B in 1988.

Another Inn at Burg's Landing recipe:
Best of Show Lemon Bread, page 56

Cranberry Crisp Coffeecake

Ingredients:

   1/3 cup butter
   1 cup old-fashioned rolled oats
   1 cup nuts, ground
   1/2 cup wheat germ, millet or rice flour
   1/2 cup honey or fruit concentrate (such as Hain's, available in health food stores)
   2 cups fresh or frozen cranberries
   1-1/2 cups water

> With a pastry blender, cut butter into small particles.
> Add oats, nuts and wheat germ. Mix butter in well.
> Stir in 1/4 cup honey.
> Place half of the mixture in a greased 8 x 8-inch baking pan. Press into place as you would a pie crust.
> Put the washed cranberries into a one-quart saucepan and cover with the water.
> Bring to a boil and boil for about 5 minutes. Remove from heat as soon as berries begin to pop.
> Drain the juice off the cranberries ("Save the cranberry juice to drink. If you mix it with a little apple juice, it is delicious.")
> Add remaining honey to the cooked berries.
> Pour cranberries over the "crust" in the pan.
> Sprinkle with the remaining "crust" mixture.
> Bake in a preheated oven at 325 degrees for 25 mintues.

Makes 6-8 servings

from **Umpqua House of Oregon**
7338 Oak Hill Road
Roseburg, OR 97470
503-459-4700

"This recipe is low in fat and sugar," said Innkeeper Rhoda Mozorosky, who completely adapted a "very sweet and gooey" recipe to serve as a coffeecake at her B&B. It might be served with fresh fruit, omelettes from fresh eggs, a baked stuffed tomato and homemade muffins.

Rhoda, a former teacher, and Allen, who gets credit for most of the home remodeling and the omelettes, moved to Roseburg and bought this two-story home specifically to open as a B&B. They opened two guestrooms in 1987.

Other Umpqua House recipes:
Fruit Smoothie, page 19
Pumpkin Muffins, page 45
High Energy Fruit Balls, page 158

Morning Raspberry Cake

Ingredients:

    1 pound butter, at room temperature
    2 cups sugar
    1 cup ripe banana, mashed (about 2 bananas)
    6 eggs
    1/2 cup sour cream
    1/2 cup milk
    2 teaspoons almond or vanilla extract
    1 tablespoon baking powder
    4 cups flour
    1 cup fresh raspberries, sliced or whole

Also:

    Powdered sugar

> Cream butter and sugar until light and fluffy.
> Mix in mashed banana, then add the eggs one at a time. Mix well.
> Mix in sour cream, milk, extract and baking powder. Continue mixing until consistency is smooth.
> Add the flour and beat only until well-mixed.
> Pour half of the mixture into a greased and floured bundt (fluted tube) pan.
> Top with the raspberries.
> Cover the layer of raspberries with the remaining cake batter to "seal in" berries.
> Bake in a preheated oven at 350 degrees for 75 minutes.
> Cool cake for 10 minutes, then invert to remove from pan. Cool for another 20 minutes, dust with powdered sugar and serve.

Makes 10-12 large servings

from **The Bombay House B&B**
8490 Beck Road NE
Bainbridge Island, WA 98110
206-842-3926

Fresh island raspberries, when in season, are available by the bowl-full every day at the Bombay House. They also go into this coffeecake, one of several homebaked goodies available from 8-10 a.m. in the large country kitchen. Guests enjoy breakfast in the kitchen or on the deck, which looks down to the beach. The Bombay House was built in 1907 on half an acre of hillside, from which the ferries can be seen sailing on the Bremerton run.

Other Bombay House recipes:
English Muffin Bread, page 59
Citrus Fruit Dip, page 81
Bombay House Granola, page 150

Orange-Pineapple Braid

Ingredients:

1 tablespoon active dry yeast
1/4 cup warm water (not higher than 115 degrees)
3 cups flour
1/4 cup sugar
1/2 teaspoon salt
1 teaspoon orange rind, freshly grated
1/2 cup milk
1/4 cup butter
1 egg
1 egg white, beaten
1/4 cup almonds, sliced

Pineapple Filling:
1/4 cup sugar
1-1/2 tablespoons cornstarch
20-ounce can pineapple
   chunks (keep 1/4 cup juice)
2 teaspoons orange rind, freshly
   grated

> Dissolve yeast in warm water.
> Place flour, sugar, salt and orange rind in food processor. Pulse a few times to blend.
> Heat milk and butter together (1 minute in microwave).
> Place egg and yeast mixture on top of flour mixture. With food processor running, pour milk/butter through the feed tube in a steady stream. Process until mixture forms a ball.
> Place dough in a greased ceramic bowl; turn dough to grease both sides. Cover with a towel and let rise in a warm place until doubled, about 1 hour.
> Make Pineapple Filling: In a small saucepan, mix sugar, cornstarch and juice. Add pineapple and orange rind. Cook over medium heat, stirring constantly, until the mixture boils and thickens. Cool slightly before spreading over dough.
> Divide dough in half. Roll each half into an 8 x 10-inch rectangle.
> Place on two greased baking sheets. Spread filling over center "third" of each rectangle.
> Cut the side "thirds" into strips one-inch wide. Criss-cross strips over the filling.
> Cover. Let rise until nearly doubled, 45-60 minutes.
> Brush with egg white, sprinkle with almonds.
> Bake in a preheated oven at 350 degrees for 25 minutes.

Makes 12-14 servings

from **Romeo Inn**
295 Idaho Street
Ashland, OR 97520
503-488-0884

Guests at the Romeo Inn get away with only a light lunch, or skipping lunch all together. It's easy to see why when this yeast-braid coffeecake is one of the breakfast items on the menu.

Other Romeo Inn recipes:
Food Processor Buttermilk Scones, page 39
Eggs Artichoke, page 93
Eggs Florentine, page 96

Oregon Blueberry Coffeecake

Ingredients:

3/4 cup sugar
1/4 cup shortening
1 egg
1/2 cup milk
2 cups flour
1/2 teaspoon salt
2 teaspoons baking powder
2 cups fresh or fresh-frozen Oregon blueberries

Crumb Topping:
1/2 cup sugar
1/3 cup flour
1/2 teaspoon cinnamon
1/4 cup butter, melted
1/2 cup Oregon hazelnuts,
    crushed

> Cream sugar and shortening.
> Add egg and mix well. Stir in milk.
> In a separate bowl, sift together flour, salt and baking powder.
> Combine dry and moist ingredients.
> Gently fold in berries.
> Spread in a greased and floured 9-inch square pan or casserole dish.
> Mix topping ingredients and sprinkle over coffeecake.
> Bake in a preheated oven at 375 degrees for 45-50 minutes.

Makes 9 three-inch servings

from **Steiger Haus**
360 Wilson Street
McMinnville, OR 97128
503-472-0821

"I adapted this recipe from others in my file about 17 years ago when I moved to Oregon from Colorado, and gained access to the abundance of nuts and berries grown in the Willamette Valley," said Innkeeper Doris Steiger. She serves it with fresh berries during "the season," and loves it warm on rainy winter mornings when she's used frozen berries.

Actress Zsa Zsa Gabor was the Steigers' third guest. Children's book author Beverly Cleary also has joined Doris, husband Lynn and daughter Brooke as a breakfast guest. Opened in 1988, their three-story, contemporary cedar home is decorated with Doris' woven rugs and placemats and sheep paintings and prints, reflecting the couple's interest in raising sheep, which they did in Eastern Oregon, and fiber arts, which Doris still pursues. She also is pursuing a doctorate in education and teaches at nearby Linfield College. Lynn is the county planning director.

The B&B is within walking distance of the college and McMinnville's restaurants and shops. Many guests come to visit Yamhill County wineries.

Sour Cream Coffeecake

Ingredients:

1 cup butter, room temperature
2-3/4 cups sugar
2 eggs, beaten
2 cups sour cream
1 tablespoon vanilla extract
2 cups flour
1 tablespoon baking powder
1/2 teaspoon salt
2 cups pecans or walnuts, chopped
1 tablespoon cinnamon

> Cream the butter and 2 cups of the sugar.
> Beat in eggs, then sour cream and vanilla.
> In a separate bowl, sift together flour, baking powder and salt.
> Fold the dry ingredients into the sour cream mixture. Beat until just blended.
> In a separate bowl, mix the remaining 3/4 cup sugar with nuts and cinnamon.
> Pour half of the batter into a greased and lightly-floured 10-inch bundt (fluted tube) pan.
> Sprinkle all of the sugar-nut mixture over the top of the batter.
> Spread the rest of the batter over the sugar-nut mixture.
> Bake in a preheated oven at 350 degrees for 1 hour, or until a knife inserted in the center comes out clean.

Makes 10-14 servings

from **Blair House**
345 Blair Avenue
Friday Harbor, WA 98250
206-378-5907

This cinnamon-spiked coffeecake makes wonderful "comfort food" and the aroma it sends while baking adds to a feeling of homeyness. Innkeeper Jane Benson bakes and serves it often for guests at Blair House on San Juan Island.

Blair House was built about 1915, on what was then the outskirts of town. Now it sits amid tall firs only about four blocks from the ferry landing. It has been expanded and remodeled several times, the last of which was in 1986 when it was converted from a private home to a seven-guestroom B&B. In addition to full breakfasts, Blair House offers guests a heated swimming pool and a year 'round hot tub.

Another Blair House recipe:
Apple Morning Cake, page 25

There's only one caution when it comes to making most muffins: don't "over-mix." If you do, the muffins may be dry with tunnels inside. Otherwise, from-scratch muffins are surprisingly easy to stir up. Muffins, scones and popovers in this collection use the region's fresh or frozen fruit or have ingredients likely to be on hand all year 'round. Recipes range from variations on traditional blueberry to satisfying Ginger Pear or Rhubarb Muffins to unusual combinations like bran and sesame seed or semi-sweet chocolate and mandarin oranges.

Muffins, Scones & Popovers

Aunt Pete's Wild Blueberry Muffins

Ingredients:
    2 cups flour
    2 teaspoons baking powder
    1/4 cup butter, softened
    1/2 teaspoon salt
    2 eggs
    1 cup sugar
    1/2 cup milk
    1 teaspoon vanilla extract
    1 to 2 cups fresh or frozen wild blueberries or wild huckleberries

Also:
    Honey

> Sift together the flour, baking powder and salt.
> In a separate bowl, beat butter, eggs and sugar.
> Add the dry ingredients to the egg mixture alternately with the milk.
> Stir in vanilla.
> Fold in blueberries (if frozen, thaw and drain off all syrup).
> Pour batter in greased or lined muffin tins two-thirds full.
> Bake in a preheated oven at 350 degrees for 25 minutes.
> Serve hot with honey and butter.

Makes 12 muffins

from **Littlefield House**
401 North Howard Street
Newberg, OR 97132
503-538-9868

"When Bert was growing up," explains Elizabeth Teitzel about her husband, "he spent the summers with his Aunt Pete and Uncle Howard on their small farm in Centralia, Wash. One of his jobs was picking berries to be used for these muffins or other special treats. Sometimes more berries were eaten than made it to the kitchen. Bert loved the fresh berries almost as much as he loved these muffins. When we started the bed and breakfast, Bert asked his Aunt Pete for her recipe."

Since 1987, when Teitzels opened two guestrooms in their large home, guests have enjoyed these muffins at the family-style breakfast. Yamhill Valley honeys, jams and jellies are served with them.

Other Littlefield House recipes:
Bert's Bran Muffins, page 36
Caitlin's Cottage Cheese Fruit Delight, page 80
Elizabeth's Broiled Breakfast Sticks, page 82

Blueberry Nut Surprise

Ingredients:

2 cups flour
1/4 cup sugar
1/2 cup brown sugar, packed
2 teaspoons baking powder
1/2 teaspoon salt
1/2 teaspoon baking soda
1 teaspoon cinnamon
1/2 cup filberts (or walnuts), chopped
1/2 cup chocolate chips
1 egg
1 cup sour cream
1/2 cup buttermilk
1/3 cup shortening, melted
1 cup fresh or frozen (dry pack) blueberries

> Mix flour, sugars, baking powder, salt, soda, cinnamon, nuts and chocolate chips.
> In a separate bowl, beat egg. Add sour cream, buttermilk and melted shortening. Mix well.
> Make a "well" in the center of the dry ingredients. Add liquid ingredients and stir until flour mixture is thoroughly moistened.
> Gently fold in blueberries.
> Fill greased muffin tins two-thirds full.
> Bake in a preheated oven at 400 degrees for 20-25 minutes.

Makes 8 jumbo muffins or 16 regular muffins

from **The Smith House B&B**
415 North College Street
Newberg, OR 97132
503-538-1995

"Yamhill County is the filbert (hazelnut) growing capital of the U.S.," said Innkeeper Mary Post. "We wanted a special muffin to spotlight the fresh Oregon blueberries and filberts grown in the area. The chocolate chips add an element of surprise and our guests love them." This is still an excellent blueberry muffin without the chocolate chips.

The Smith House is in the heart of Yamhill wine country and located two blocks from George Fox College. Mary and Glen Post, Smokey the gray cat and Belvedere and Ragnavald, family dogs, opened their two-guestroom B&B in 1989. Guests get a special kick out of talking with Tequilla, an Amazon parrot, and rave about the hot tub located outside in an enclosed patio.

Bert's Bran Muffins

Ingredients:

3 heaping cups bran
9/10 cup honey
1 cup flour
1-1/2 cups whole wheat flour
2-1/2 teaspoons baking soda
1/2 teaspoon salt
2 eggs, slightly beaten
1/2 cup vegetable oil
2 cups buttermilk

> Mix all ingredients thoroughly.
> Pour batter into greased or lined muffin tins two-thirds full.
> Bake in a preheated oven at 400 degrees for 20 minutes.
> Refrigerate unused batter. It will keep for up to six weeks in the refrigerator.

Makes 24 muffins

from **Littlefield House**
401 North Howard Street
Newberg, OR 97132
503-538-9868

Innkeeper Bert Teitzel has made these muffins one of his specialties. He doubles the recipe and then uses the refrigerated batter to make fresh muffins every morning for guests. They are equally tasty spread with honey, jams or jellies, he reports.

Bert and Elizabeth opened two guestrooms in their 1909 home in the heart of Oregon wine country. In addition to his bran muffins, Bert's pride and joy is his classic cars. And like his bran muffins, he shares them with guests. Guests are offered chauffeured wine tasting tours in the vintage limos, a '57 Mercedes limousine, a '56 Cadillac limousine, and a '47 Buick Roadmaster. The popular package, which means guests don't have to think about driving in unfamiliar territory, especially after wine tasting, includes a gourmet picnic lunch and dinner at one of the county's finest restaurants.

The more than 20 wineries within a half-hour drive of Newberg is one reason people come to town. Antiquing is another. Several antique shops are within walking distance of the Littlefield House.

Other Littlefield House recipes:
Aunt Pete's Wild Blueberry Muffins, page 34
Caitlin's Cottage Cheese Fruit Delight, page 80
Elizabeth's Broiled Breakfast Sticks, page 82

Bran Muffins with Sesame Seed

Ingredients:

1/4 cup shortening
1/2 cup brown sugar, packed
1/4 cup honey
3 eggs, beaten
1 cup milk
1-1/2 cups bran cereal
1 cup flour
2 teaspoons baking powder
1/2 teaspoon baking soda
1/2 teaspoon salt
1/2 cup raisins

Also:

Extra honey
Sesame seeds

> Combine shortening, brown sugar, honey and eggs. Then add milk and bran.
> In a separate bowl, mix flour, baking powder, soda, salt and raisins.
> Add dry to liquid ingredients. Stir just to mix well.
> Spray 18 muffin cups with a non-stick coating.
> Into each cup, place 1 teaspoon honey and sprinkle with sesame seeds.
> Add batter until each cup is two-thirds full.
> Bake in a preheated oven at 400 degrees for 15-20 minutes.

Makes 18 muffins

from **Mildred's B&B**
1201 15th Avenue E.
Seattle, WA 98112
206-325-6072

"The addition of honey and sesame seed makes these outstanding," said Innkeeper Mildred Sarver, whose guests often like to linger over another muffin and conversation with their hostess. Mildred opened her home, directly across from Volunteer Park on Capitol Hill, in 1982 with three guestrooms. It is a family home and it has been transformed into comfortable lodging in the heart of the city.

Other Mildred's B&B recipes:
No-Crust Smoked Salmon Quiche, page 100
Grandma Jessie Bell's Scotch Shortbread, page 156

Choco-Mandarin Muffins

Ingredients:
    1 11-ounce can mandarin oranges
    2 cups flour
    2 teaspoons baking powder
    1/2 teaspoon baking soda
    1/2 teaspoon salt
    1/4 cup sugar
    1/2 cup brown sugar, packed
    1 egg, beaten
    1 cup sour cream
    1/2 cup shortening, melted
    1/4 cup filberts, ground
    1/2 cup semi-sweet chocolate chips

> Drain orange segments, saving liquid. Put segments in a measuring cup. Add liquid to make 8 ounces.
> In a large bowl, combine flour, baking powder, soda, salt and sugars.
> In a separate bowl, stir together egg, sour cream, oranges and melted shortening.
> Make a "well" in the center of the dry ingredients. Add egg mixture, nuts and chocolate chips. Stir just until all ingredients are moistened.
> Spoon batter into 12 greased muffin cups, dividing batter evenly between them.
> Bake in a preheated oven at 400 degrees for 20-25 minutes.

Makes 12 large muffins

from **North Garden Inn**
1014 North Garden Street
Bellingham, WA 98225
206-671-7828

Chocolate is not unusual in the baked goods on Barbara and Frank DeFreytas' breakfast table, much to the delight of guests, who might not so indulge at home. They've even won contests with their recipes. (One of their secrets: Barbara grinds her own flour from the 50-pound sacks of wheat she buys.)

Barb and Frank bought and remodeled this huge 1897 Queen Anne home, saving the 51 windows but removing several of the five apartment kitchens. They opened 10 guestrooms and five baths in 1986. The home was built as a private residence, but had been turned into apartments in the 1940s. Barb, a former drama teacher and church staff member, and Frank, a piano and voice teacher, decided the home would make a fine B&B and have room for a studio for Frank, as well. Guests may now enjoy the two grand pianos and occasional sing-alongs or musical dramas, encouraged to join by the hosts.

Food Processor Buttermilk Scones

Ingredients:
>1/2 cup raisins
>2 cups flour
>1/3 cup sugar
>1-1/2 teaspoons baking powder
>1/2 teaspoon baking soda
>1/4 teaspoon salt
>6 tablespoons butter, chilled and cut into 1-inch chunks
>1/2 cup buttermilk
>1 egg
>1 teaspoon vanilla extract

Also:
>2 tablespoons buttermilk
>Sugar

> Plump raisins in hot water for 5-10 minutes, then drain on paper towels.
> In food processor, blend flour, sugar, baking powder, soda and salt by pulsing a few times.
> Add butter chunks and process about 30 seconds until well blended.
> In a large measuring cup, mix the buttermilk, egg and vanilla.
> Pour milk mixture into the food processor in a steady stream while processing; stop when the liquid has been absorbed.
> Transfer dough to a well-floured board. Spread raisins on top. Sprinkle with additional flour and knead 15-30 seconds.
> Roll dough into an 8-inch circle. Cut into eight wedges (or use a heart cookie cutter).
> Place scones one inch apart on a lightly-greased baking sheet.
> Brush with buttermilk and sprinkle with sugar.
> Bake in a preheated oven at 400 degrees for 13-15 minutes, until lightly browned.

Makes 8 scones

from **Romeo Inn**
295 Idaho Street
Ashland, OR 97520
503-488-0884

"This recipe is *so* easy, but a favorite of many of our guests," says Innkeeper Margaret Halverson. "The scones are light and fluffy." Scones often are part of a hearty breakfast in the dining room of this 1930s Cape Cod home, set amid 300-year-old Ponderosa pines (there's a hammock hanging between two of them). Margaret and Bruce have six guestrooms in their B&B.

Other Romeo Inn recipes:
Orange-Pineapple Braid, page 29
Eggs Artichoke, page 93
Eggs Florentine, page 96

Ginger Pear Muffins

Ingredients:

2 cups flour
1/2 cup brown sugar, packed
1 teaspoon baking soda
1/2 teaspoon salt
2 teaspoons ginger
1/8 teaspoon cloves
1/8 teaspoon nutmeg
1 cup plain yogurt
1/2 cup vegetable oil
3 tablespoons molasses
1 egg, beaten
1-1/2 cups fresh, unpeeled pears, diced
1/2 cup raisins
1/2 cup nuts, chopped

> Mix flour, brown sugar, soda, salt and spices in a large bowl.
> In a separate bowl, mix yogurt, oil, molasses and egg.
> Fold liquid ingredients into dry, mixing just until dry ingredients are moistened.
> Stir in pears, raisins and nuts.
> Spoon batter into greased or lined muffin tins two-thirds full.
> Bake in a preheated oven at 400 degrees for 20 minutes.

Makes 12-18 muffins

from **Salisbury House**
750 16th Avenue E.
Seattle, WA 98112
206-328-8682

If you think the aroma of baking cinnamon and apples is tempting, you haven't discovered ginger and pears. "This recipe started as a cinnamon-apple muffin recipe," said Innkeeper Cathryn Wiese, "but we have a wonderful pear tree at Salisbury House, so I changed the fruit to pears and thought ginger a better companion for them. Voila!" The molasses was an inspired addition, and yogurt keeps them moist.

In 1985, Cathryn and co-innkeeper/mother Mary opened four guestrooms in their large, light and airy Capitol Hill home, which is close to Volunteer Park. Summer guests particularly enjoy a glass of lemonade on the wrap-around porch of the turn-of-the-century home.

Other Salisbury House recipes:
Whole Wheat Irish Soda Bread, page 66
South of the Border Quiche, page 105
Mary's Citrus French Toast, page 108

Golden Raisin Scones

Ingredients:

3-1/4 cups flour
4 teaspoons cream of tartar
2 teaspoons baking soda
1 teaspoon salt
6 tablespoons butter, chilled
1 cup golden raisins
3 tablespoons sugar
1 cup milk

> Mix flour, cream of tartar, soda and salt together in a large bowl.
> Cut in butter with a pastry blender until the mixture resembles coarse meal.
> Add raisins and sugar. Then mix in enough milk to make a soft dough.
> Put dough on a floured surface and knead *gently*, just until the dough holds together.
> Pat out to a half-inch thick. Cut out with cookie cutter or the rim of a juice glass.
> Arrange on a floured baking sheet and dust tops with flour.
> Bake in a preheated oven at 425 degrees for 10 minutes. Serve hot.

Makes 12-16 scones

from **Marit's B&B**
6208 Palatine Avenue N.
Seattle, WA 98103
206-782-7900

"These scones are a great favorite. Guests who stay for any length of time will ask for re-runs of these," promises Innkeeper Marit Nelson, who loves these served hot with lots of butter and raspberry jam. The recipe came straight from Britain via a friend.

Marit herself was born in Norway, and the B&B she and husband Carl run in their brick Tudor home may be as close to the European concept as one will find in this country. This is the home where they raised five children, now grown. "I went to college to get a new career and dropped out after three years," Marit said, explaining that she had been in preparation for innkeeping for 25 years, during which time she mothered. Now her table often is full again, giving her a chance to cook up a storm.

Other Marit's B&B recipes:
Norwegian Pancakes with Lingonberry Cream, page 119
Good and Good-for-You Yummie Cookies, page 155

Maryellen's Magic Muffins

Ingredients:

1 cup orange juice
Rind from 1 orange, grated
1/4 cup canola oil
1/2 cup honey
1 egg
1-1/2 cups whole wheat pastry flour
1/2 cup oat bran
2 teaspoons baking powder
1/2 teaspoon salt
1 teaspoon cinnamon
1 cup ripe banana, mashed
1/2 cup "nutty" granola

> Combine juice, rind, oil, honey and egg in a large bowl.
> In a separate bowl, mix flour, oat bran, baking powder, salt and cinnamon.
> Add dry ingredients and mashed banana alternately to the liquid mixture.
> Divide batter between 12 lined or greased muffin tins.
> Sprinkle granola on top of each muffin.
> Bake in a preheated oven at 375 degrees for 25-30 minutes.

Makes 12 large muffins

from **Maryellen's Guest House**
1583 Fircrest
Eugene, OR 97403
503-342-7375

Maryellen calls her muffins "magic" because of their healthful high fiber, low fat ingredients. The muffins are served warm from the oven with fresh Oregon fruit and a yogurt compote. Guests may breakfast in their own room, on their private deck or in the dining room of this modern hillside home.

In 1988, Maryellen and Bob Larson opened two guestrooms in their home, located three minutes from the University of Oregon. Guests are welcome to enjoy the outdoor pool and whirlpool hot tub.

Maryellen and Bob, who dated in high school, met again at their 25-year high school reunion and they married six months later. Bob is a bakery distributor in Eugene, and Maryellen, who formerly worked in marketing, operates the B&B. "I love taking care of people and visiting with folks from all over the country," she noted.

Melinda's Whole Wheat Blueberry Muffins

Ingredients:

2 cups whole wheat flour (or 1 cup whole wheat and 1 cup unbleached flour)
2 teaspoons baking powder
1/2 teaspoon cinnamon
1/2 teaspoon salt
1 egg, beaten
1 cup water
3 tablespoons vegetable oil
2 to 4 tablespoons honey
1 to 1-1/2 cups fresh or frozen (dry pack) blueberries

> Mix flour, baking powder, cinnamon and salt.
> Add egg, water, oil and honey. Stir together just until mixed.
> Fill greased or lined muffin tins half full.
> Bake in a preheated oven at 375 degrees for 15-20 minutes.

Makes 16 muffins

from **Spring Creek Llama Ranch**
14700 NE Spring Creek Lane
Newberg, OR 97132
503-538-5717

This recipe was developed by Innkeeper Melinda Van Bossuyt, partly to take advantage of Oregon's wonderful blueberry harvest, and partly to create a healthy muffin without butter or milk ("Very rarely do dairy products, soy or pork enter my cooking," she said, and she caters to B&B guests' dietary restrictions, too). The blueberries used are home-grown.

Melinda and Dave not only have a two guestroom B&B on their 24-acre llama ranch in Oregon's wine country, but they offer B&B — "Barn & Breakfast" — for traveling llamas, as well. They find that most of their human guests arrive llama-less, but are eager to learn more about the gentle beasts. Van Bossuyts gladly oblige, and the llamas "come to the fence and greet newcomers with a sniff and a kiss."

Guests who prefer to socialize with each other can walk in the woods surrounding the house, check for fresh eggs in the hen house, or enjoy Newberg's antique shops and wineries.

Other Spring Creek Llama Ranch recipes:
Naturally Sweet Fruit Syrup, page 72
Melinda's Famous Wholegrain Waffles, page 122
Our Favorite Oatmeal-Raisin Cookie, page 160

Old-Fashioned Popovers

Ingredients:

1 cup flour (or 1/2 cup unbleached flour and 1/2 cup oatmeal or whole wheat flour)
1/2 teaspoon salt
2 eggs, beaten
1 cup milk
1 tablespoon butter, melted

Also:

Apple butter, marmalade or preserves

> Grease muffin pans with plenty of shortening.
> Place prepared pans in an oven which has been preheated to 450 degrees. Remove sizzling hot pans only when ready to fill with popover batter.
> For the batter, beat all ingredients together. ("You cannot beat the batter too much.")
> Quickly pour batter into hot muffin tins one-third full.
> Bake at 450 degrees for 15 minutes, then reduce heat to 350 degrees and continue baking for about 5 minutes. Poke a small hole in each popover to let steam escape, and continue baking for about 10 minutes, until popovers are golden brown and puffed.
> Serve hot with apple butter, marmalade or favorite preserves.

Makes 6 large popovers

from **The Sylvan Haus**
417 Wilder Hill Drive
P.O. Box 416
Montesano, WA 98563
206-249-3453

Innkeeper JoAnne Murphy was given this treasured recipe by her grandmother, who passed on scores of recipes handwritten on scraps of paper and old envelopes. JoAnne now serves the popovers to B&B guests.

JoAnne and Mike, who have retired from the drugstore business, have three guestrooms in their contemporary home. Guests dine on these popovers, along with pancakes or another entree, in the two-story dining room, surrounded by windows. The home boasts five decks (it has as many bedrooms) and guests are welcome to use the outdoor hot tub on one of the decks. The home is surrounded by tall pines on Wilder Hill.

Guests find themselves only a five-minute hike to Lake Sylvia State Park for swimming, boating and fishing. Aberdeen and its tall ships moored in Grays Harbor are a 15-minute drive from the B&B.

Pumpkin Muffins

Ingredients:

1/2 cup vegetable oil
1 cup cooked (fresh or canned) pumpkin
2 eggs, slightly beaten
1 teaspoon vanilla extract
1/2 cup honey, fruit concentrate (such as Hain's), or frozen apple juice concentrate
1 cup unsweetened applesauce
1-7/8 cups whole wheat flour (1/2 cup oat bran may be substituted for part of flour)
1 teaspoon cinnamon
1/2 teaspoon nutmeg
1/2 teaspoon allspice
1/4 teaspoon ginger
1 teaspoon baking soda
1 cup raisins, soaked in apple juice or whiskey (reserve 1/4 cup of liquid)
1 cup walnuts, chopped

> In a large bowl, mix oil, pumpkin, eggs, vanilla, honey and applesauce.
> In a separate bowl, sift together flour, spices and baking soda.
> Add dry ingredients to pumpkin mixture and stir just until mixed.
> Stir in raisins, 1/4 cup of reserved liquid and nuts.
> Fill 12 paper-lined muffin tins two-thirds full.
> Bake in a preheated oven at 325 degrees for 30 minutes.

Makes 12 large muffins

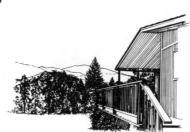

from **Umpqua House of Oregon**
7338 Oak Hill Road
Roseburg, OR 97470
503-459-4700

Innkeeper Rhoda Mozorosky swapped a zucchini bread recipe for this one, then adapted it to her own needs. She changed the amount of oil, removed the sugar, substituted flours, added the applesauce and was inspired to soak the raisins. Guests love the muffins hot, and no one can complain about unhealthy ingredients. (Even the eggs are fresh from their own chickens, happily and organically raised on the 6.5 acres.)

Other Umpqua House recipes:
Fruit Smoothie, page 19
Cranberry Crisp Coffeecake, page 27
High Energy Fruit Balls, page 158

Raspberry Muffins

Ingredients:

1-1/2 cups flour
1/4 cup sugar
1/4 cup brown sugar, packed
2 teaspoons baking powder
2 teaspoons orange zest (rind), grated
1/4 teaspoon cinnamon
1 egg, beaten
1/2 cup butter, melted
1/2 cup milk
1-1/2 cups fresh or frozen (dry pack)* raspberries
   *If frozen raspberries are used, first add 2 tablespoons flour to the berries

Topping:
1/2 cup nuts, chopped
1/2 cup brown sugar, packed
1/4 cup flour
1 teaspoon cinnamon
1 teaspoon orange zest, grated

> In a large bowl, combine flour, sugars, baking powder, orange zest and cinnamon.
> Combine egg, butter and milk. Pour mixture into a "well" in the dry ingredients.
> Stir gently with a wooden spoon just until mixed. Don't overmix.
> Gently fold in raspberries.
> Fill greased or lined muffin tins three-quarters full.
> For Topping: Combine all ingredients. Sprinkle over tops of muffins.
> Bake in a preheated oven at 350 degrees for 20-25 minutes.

Makes 12 muffins

from **Eagles Nest Inn**
3236 East Saratoga Road
Langley, WA 98260
206-321-5331

Innkeeper Nancy Bowman modified a friend's recipe and now has wonderful warm muffins to serve with an egg dish to her B&B guests. Guests are served breakfast in the bright country kitchen or outside on the deck, both of which overlook Saratoga Passage. But either way, it's served family-style. "We believe that it is the essence of the B&B experience, when everyone comes together to share travel stories and friendship. We've had several people develop and continue friendships after meeting here," Nancy said.

Nancy and Dale designed and built this octagon-shaped home, which they constructed specifically as a B&B, and opened three guestrooms in 1987. The B&B is located up a winding road amid tall spruces, about a mile-and-a-half from the village of Langley.

Other Eagles Nest Inn recipes:
Ricotta Cheese Pancakes, page 120
Chip 'n Dale Chocolate Chip Cookies, page 153

Rhubarb Muffins

Ingredients:

1-1/4 cups brown sugar, packed
1/2 cup vegetable oil
1 egg
2 teaspoons vanilla extract
1 cup buttermilk
1-1/2 cups fresh or frozen rhubarb, diced
1/2 cup walnuts, chopped
2 cups flour
1/2 cup wheat germ
1 teaspoon baking soda
1 teaspoon baking powder
1/2 teaspoon salt

Topping:
1/3 cup sugar
1 teaspoon cinnamon
1 tablespoon butter, melted

> Mix brown sugar and vegetable oil. Add egg, vanilla and buttermilk.
> Stir in rhubarb and nuts.
> In a separate bowl, mix flour, wheat germ, soda, baking powder and salt.
> Combine the dry ingredients with the rhubarb mixture and stir just until blended.
> Spoon into greased or lined muffin tins two-thirds full.
> Top with sugar/cinnamon/butter mixture.
> Bake in a preheated oven at 400 degrees for 20-25 minutes.

Makes 12 muffins

from **The Clinkerbrick House**
2311 NE Schuyler Street
Portland, OR 97212
503-281-2533

Innkeeper Peggie Irvine whips up these muffins using fresh spring rhubarb, and they may accompany specialty omelettes for breakfast. Guests are served in the bright dining room by the bay window and leaded glass china cupboard, original to this 1908 Dutch Colonial home in a nice Northeast neighborhood.

The most unusual part of the home is on the outside: the original builder used "clinker" bricks — the ones that came out of the furnace wildly distorted and unsaleable — for its brick front. Peggie and Bob bought the house to open a B&B. Bob, who owns a custom drapery business, had run out of handyman projects to complete on their former home of 21 years.

Another Clinkerbrick House recipe:
Breakfast Pretzels, page 57

Sesame Corn Muffins

Ingredients:

3/4 cup unbleached flour
3/4 cup whole wheat flour
1/2 cup sugar
1-1/2 teaspoons salt
1-1/4 teaspoons baking soda
2 cups cornmeal
1 cup wheat germ
1/2 cup sesame seeds, toasted
2 cups buttermilk
3/4 cup butter, melted
2 eggs, slightly beaten

> In a large bowl, sift together flours, sugar, salt and soda. Stir in cornmeal, wheat germ and sesame seeds.
> Mix buttermilk, butter and eggs on medium speed in a blender or with an egg beater until thoroughly blended.
> Pour milk mixture into dry ingredients. Stir just until moistened. Do not overmix.
> Pour into greased or lined muffin tins two-thirds full.
> Bake in a preheated oven at 350 degrees for 30 minutes.

Makes 14-18 muffins

from **Turtleback Farm Inn**
Crow Valley Road
Route 1, Box 650
Orcas Island, WA 98245
206-376-4914

These muffins often are served hot as part of a bountiful home-cooked breakfast served in this farmhouse dining room. Innkeepers Susan and Bill Fletcher are no more about to skimp on breakfast than they were on renovation of a rundown farmhouse, expanding to seven guestrooms, or comfortable and cozy country decor.

Fletchers, who were living in northern California, came to Orcas in 1984, looking for a summer home. What they got was an architect-designed house on 80 rolling acres plus the original turn-of-the-century farmhouse that was being used to store hay. Rather than tearing the farmhouse down, they decided to renovate and enter innkeeping on the island full time.

Other Turtleback Farm Inn recipes:
Souffle Roll, page 104
Cornmeal Waffles, page 121
Applesauce Bread Pudding, page 143

Singing Hinnies (Currant Scones)

Ingredients:

2 cups flour
1 tablespoon baking powder
1/2 teaspoon baking soda
1 teaspoon salt
1/4 cup cold vegetable shortening, cut into pieces
1/4 cup cold unsalted butter, cut into pieces
1/3 cup dried currants
2 tablespoons sour cream
3/4 cup milk
1 egg, beaten
1 teaspoon water

English Cream:
1/4 teaspoon mace
1/4 cup powdered sugar
1 cup heavy cream
2 tablespoons lemon rind, grated
2/3 cup sour cream

> For English Cream: Sift powdered sugar and mace into heavy cream, then beat in lemon rind. Beat until stiff peaks form. Gently fold in sour cream. Cover and chill for 1 hour.
> Sift together flour, baking powder, soda and salt. Blend in shortening and butter until mixture resembles coarse meal.
> Stir in currants.
> In a separate bowl, beat together the sour cream and milk.
> Add milk mixture to dry ingredients. Stir with a fork until it forms a dough.
> Knead on a lightly-floured board for 30 seconds. Pat into a round about 3/4-inch thick.
> Transfer dough to a greased 8-inch cake or pie pan. Pat top smooth.
> Mix egg with water. Brush "egg wash" on top of scone dough. Score top with a knife into eight wedges.
> Bake in a preheated oven at 400 degrees for 25-30 minutes, until golden brown.
> Cool in pan for 5 minutes. Turn out onto rack. Cut into wedges. Split each scone crosswise and pile each half with English Cream.

Makes 8 scones and 2 cups English Cream

from **Westwinds B&B**
4909-H Hannah Highlands Road
Friday Harbor, WA 98250
206-378-5283

Eight hearty scones are more than guests usually can finish off here, because Innkeepers Christine Durbin and Gayle Rollins have one suite for only two pampered guests at a time. Christine and Gayle opened their "wilderness spot" in 1988. The contemporary hilltop home takes advantage of a 180-degree view of the Strait of Juan de Fuca, the Olympic Mountains and Victoria, B.C. Guests may enjoy breakfast on their private deck.

Another Westwinds B&B recipe:
Blackberry Cobbler, page 144

Super Cornmeal Muffins

Ingredients:

1-1/2 cups flour
1/2 cup whole wheat flour
1 cup yellow cornmeal
4-1/2 teaspoons baking powder
3 tablespoons sugar
1/4 teaspoon salt
2 eggs, lightly beaten
1 cup buttermilk
1 cup small curd cottage cheese
1/3 cup vegetable oil

> In a large bowl, mix flours, cornmeal, baking powder, sugar and salt (do not sift flours).
> In a separate bowl, mix eggs, buttermilk, cottage cheese and oil.
> Make a "well" in the center of the dry ingredients. Pour egg mixture into the well and stir only until all ingredients are moist.
> Spoon into greased muffin tins until two-thirds full.
> Bake in a preheated oven at 400 degrees for 20 minutes.

Makes 24 muffins

from **General Hooker's House**
125 SW Hooker Street
Portland, OR 97201
503-222-4435

"I am mad about cornmeal," said Innkeeper Lori Hall, "and the cottage cheese makes these muffins beautifully moist." She serves them often to guests, who dine around her grandmother's huge oak table in this Portland B&B.

Lori bought this 1888 Queen Anne Victorian home, renovated it herself and opened four guest rooms in 1986. The house had "suffered neglect, abuse and a serious fire," Lori said, before its "massive rehabilitation project." Located in a quiet, gentrifying neighborhood that also is an Historic Conservation District, it's named after the man for whom the street was named. He was "Fighting Joe" Hooker, a Union general from Massachusetts and one of several Civil War generals immortalized in street names when the neighborhood was platted in 1875. While General Hooker obviously never slept here, Lori's cat is named "General Hooker," so, she says, "it truly is General Hooker's House."

Another General Hooker's House recipe:
Apricot Banana Nut Bread, page 54

Yogurt Scones

Ingredients:
2 cups flour
1/4 teaspoon salt, optional
1/2 teaspoon baking soda
2 teaspoons baking powder
2 tablespoons sugar
6 tablespoons butter
1 egg, separated
1 cup plain yogurt
1/2 to 3/4 cup raisins, optional
2 teaspoons sugar
1/4 teaspoon cinnamon

> In a large bowl, mix flour, salt, soda, baking powder and sugar.
> Cut in the butter as for pie crust, until mixture is crumbly. Make a "well" in the center.
> Pour the egg yolk, yogurt and raisins into the "well." Mix lightly until well blended.
> Turn dough out onto a floured surface. Knead lightly 12 times.
> Pat dough out to a half-inch thick. Cut into circles with a 3-inch cookie or biscuit cutter. Place circles on an ungreased cookie sheet.
> Using a sharp knife dusted with flour, cut the circles into four wedges.
> In a small bowl, beat the egg white slightly. Brush onto the dough.
> Mix the sugar and cinnamon and sprinkle on top of the dough.
> Bake in a preheated oven at 425 degrees for 14 -18 minutes. Cool slightly, but serve warm.

Makes 20-25 scones

from **St. Helens Manorhouse**
7476 U.S. Highway 12
Morton, WA 98356
206-498-5243

Innkeeper Darlene Brown's recipe "is easy to make in the morning and not as sweet as muffins," she said. They often are part of a full, all-you-can-eat country breakfast served family-style in this 1910 home, which was built of Douglas fir and first used as roadside lodging for peddlers and travelers.

In 1985, Darlene and Jack Brown bought and remodeled the three-story home, located six miles from Morton at the 1,000 foot level. Today it is popular as a "home base" for those exploring Mt. St. Helens or Mt. Rainier. Browns offer four guestrooms, which have fresh flowers from the outdoor plants every day in the summer.

Any way you slice it, absolutely *nothing* beats the smell of bread baking on a damp or chilly morning. Well, perhaps the smell of cinnamon rolls baking. Some recipes for rolls and breads with yeast, requiring time to "rise," are included. Several recipes are for sweet breads that can be whipped up in just a few minutes. And many of those are so moist and flavorful they require no butter ing. What's more, innovative innkeepers found ways to add the bounty of the Pacific Northwest — such as hazelnuts, strawberries or huckleberries — to their bread recipes.

Breads

Apricot Banana Nut Bread

Ingredients:

    2 cups flour
    1 cup sugar
    1/2 cup dried apricots, chopped or snipped
    1/2 cup walnuts, chopped
    1 teaspoon baking powder
    1/2 teaspoon salt
    1/2 teaspoon baking soda
    1 egg, slightly beaten
    1/2 cup milk
    1/4 cup butter or margarine, melted
    3/4 cup very ripe banana, mashed

> In a large bowl, mix the first seven ingredients.
> In a separate bowl, mix egg, milk, butter and banana.
> Pour egg mixture into the dry ingredients and stir only until all ingredients are moist.
> Pour batter into a greased 9-inch loaf pan.
> Bake in a preheated oven at 350 degrees for 60-90 minutes, or until a toothpick inserted in the center comes out clean.

Makes 1 loaf

from **General Hooker's House**
125 SW Hooker Street
Portland, OR 97201
503-222-4435

This fruit nut bread is often part of the breakfasts Innkeeper Lori Hall serves family-style in her 1888 Queen Anne Victorian home. Summer guests often take their breakfast out the French doors from the dining room onto the deck. Because the home is in a quiet historic neighborhood only a bus ride or walk from the heart of downtown, it attracts both business and pleasure travelers.

Lori bought this house, which was on the verge of demolition, for a B&B and opened four guestrooms in 1986. On the outside, it has landscaped grounds, clapboard siding with gingerbread, and tastefully-painted trim. Inside, rooms are decorated with antiques, rattan and family heirlooms. There are high ceilings and plenty of windows, so the rooms are light and airy.

Lori, a native Portlander, helps travelers plan to explore her city. A roof-top deck with a city view is for guests' use. An upscale deli is around the corner and the Metro YMCA and parks are only blocks away.

Another General Hooker's House recipe:
Super Cornmeal Muffins, page 50

Banana Mango Loaf

Ingredients:

1/2 cup margarine
1/2 cup sugar
1/2 cup light brown sugar, packed
2 ripe bananas
Pulp from 1 ripe mango
2 eggs
3 tablespoons buttermilk
1 teaspoon baking soda
2 cups flour (unbleached preferred)
1/2 cup pecans

Also:

Oatmeal
Sugar
Cinnamon

> Butter a loaf pan with margarine. Sprinkle lightly with oatmeal, sugar and cinnamon.
> In a food processor, cream margarine and sugars.
> Add fruit, eggs and buttermilk. Process until blended.
> Add soda and flour and blend well.
> Pour in the nuts. (They will be chopped by the food processor.)
> Pour batter into the prepared pan. Bake in a preheated oven at 325 degrees for 1 hour.

Makes 1 loaf

from **The Gallery B&B at
Little Cape Horn**
4 Little Cape Horn
Cathlamet, WA 98612
206-425-7395

"I had a good banana bread recipe, but one day I was short one banana, so I substituted an available mango and enjoyed the additional flavor," said Innkeeper Carolyn Feasey, who confesses to also using applesauce instead of that extra banana. "The oatmeal makes a nice crispy crust."

Guests at this river- and beach-front B&B often enjoy a beach walk in between breakfast courses, making the meal a long-savored event. Carolyn and Eric opened guestrooms in 1985 for guests who are hooked on the Columbia River, nearby Pacific Ocean or both. Their contemporary home has many windows and decks for drinking in the views.

Other Gallery B&B recipes:
Homemade Hollandaise, page 69
Eggs Benedict in Puff Pastry, page 94

Best of Show Lemon Bread

Ingredients:

1 cup sugar
1/3 cup butter, melted
1 tablespoon lemon extract
2 eggs
1-1/2 cups sifted flour
1 teaspoon baking powder
1 teaspoon salt
1/2 cup milk
Peel from 1 large lemon, grated
1/2 cup nuts, chopped

Glaze:
   Juice of 1 large lemon
     (2-3 tablespoons)
   1/3 cup sugar

> In a large bowl, cream sugar, butter, lemon extract and eggs.
> In a separate bowl, combine the flour, baking powder and salt.
> Stir the dry ingredients into the egg mixture alternately with the milk.
> Mix in lemon peel and nuts.
> Pour into a greased loaf pan. Bake in a preheated oven at 350 degrees for 45-60 minutes or until a knife inserted in the center comes out clean.
> For Glaze: While bread is baking, mix juice and sugar .
> With a toothpick, poke small holes in the warm bread immediately after removing it from the oven.
> Drizzle glaze over the top of the warm bread. Let the bread sit overnight. Serve cold.

Makes 1 loaf

from **The Inn at Burg's Landing**
8808 Villa Beach Road
Anderson Island, WA 98303
206-884-9185

This moist bread recipe took "best of show" in 1988 at the Evergreen State Fair for Innkeeper Annie Burg. She has been making it for years as "an old family recipe," and now serves it to B&B guests, who agree it's a winner.

Annie and Ken's log home also gets raves. Built in 1987 of local logs, it overlooks the ferry landing and Puget Sound with a picture-window view of Mt. Rainier. Burgs ancestors pioneered in 1889 on Anderson Island. "The Burg family has always participated in the social activities of the island, such as the annual fair, quilting bees, basket parties, salmon bakes and the volunteer firemens' pancake breakfast," said Annie. Now they help guests explore and enjoy the island's biking, golfing and Lake Josephine.

Another Inn at Burg's Landing recipe:
Applesauce Coffee Braid, page 26

Breakfast Pretzels

Ingredients:

1 package active dry yeast
1 tablespoon sugar
1 teaspoon salt
1-1/2 cups warm water (not higher than 115 degrees)
4 cups flour
1/2 cup raisins

Topping:
1 egg, beaten
1/3 cup sugar
1 teaspoon cinnamon

> Dissolve yeast, salt and sugar in warm water.
> Add yeast mixture to flour. Mix in raisins.
> Knead dough until smooth.
> Cut dough into eight pieces and roll each piece by hand into a rope. Twist each rope into the desired shape.
> Place pretzels on a lightly greased cookie sheet.
> Brush pretzels with the beaten egg. Sprinkle with sugar-cinnamon mixture.
> Bake in a preheated oven at 425 degrees for about 12-15 minutes.

Makes 8 large pretzels

from **The Clinkerbrick House**
2311 NE Schuyler Street
Portland, OR 97212
503-281-2533

"Breakfast Pretzels are easy and quick to make — there's no need to allow extra time for rising," said Innkeeper Peggie Irvine. These may *look* like traditional pretzels, but with raisins and sugar-cinnamon topping, they are definitely a breakfast treat that doesn't resemble the salty snack.

Peggie and Bob opened this 1908 Dutch Colonial home with "clinker" bricks on the front as a B&B in 1987. The three guestrooms are upstairs, decorated in antiques. Guests have a private entrance and have the option of using a fully-equipped kitchen, handy if their stay in Portland is a long one.

The Clinkerbrick House is located one block from shopping and restaurants on NE Broadway. It's close to the "MAX" light rail system, the Lloyd Center, Convention Center and Memorial Coliseum. "Breakfast time is my favorite time, visiting with our guests and helping them plan their day," said Peggie.

Another Clinkerbrick House recipe:
Rhubarb Muffins, page 47

Cinnamon Swirls

Ingredients:

1/2 cup sugar
2 teaspoons salt
1 cup butter, cut in pieces
1 cup boiling water
1 cup warm water (no higher than 115 degrees)
2 packages active dry yeast
2 eggs, at room temperature (don't leave out
    of the refrigerator for more than two hours)
6 cups flour

Also:

Vegetable oil
Walnuts, chopped

Filling for 1/4 of dough:
1/4 cup butter, soft
3 tablespoons sugar
1/3 cup raisins
1 teaspoon cinnamon
Icing for 1/4 of recipe:
1/2 cup powdered sugar
4 teaspoons milk
1/2 teaspoon vanilla extract

> In a large bowl, mix sugar, salt, butter and boiling water. Stir until the butter is melted.
> In a two-cup measuring cup, dissolve yeast in warm water.
> When ingredients in the large bowl have cooled, add eggs, water and yeast, and the flour, one cup at a time. Beat well.
> Place dough in an oiled bowl that is large enough to accommodate rising dough.
> Cover with a towel and refrigerate at least 5 hours (will keep in refrigerator for 4 days).
> Oil hands, rolling pin and rolling surface with vegetable oil. Then roll out a quarter of the dough to an 11 x 17-inch rectangle. (Cover and refrigerate remaining dough.)
> Spread with the filling ingredients.
> Roll up the dough, starting on the 17-inch side so the final roll is 17 inches long.
> Using a thin string, cut the roll into 16 equal pieces. Place on an ungreased cookie sheet.
> Place in a warm spot and let rise for 1-2 hours.
> Bake in a preheated oven at 350 degrees for 15 minutes or until light brown.
> Remove swirls to a rack. Drizzle with icing mixture. Sprinkle with chopped walnuts.
> Repeat rolling, filling, rising and baking process with rest of the dough as desired.

Makes 64 swirls

from **Olympic Lights**
4531-A Cattle Point Road
Friday Harbor, WA 98250
206-378-3186

"This is the recipe my mother chose for teaching 10-year-old 4-H girls (their first experience with yeast dough)," said Innkeeper Lea Andrade. "If you keep your hands oiled, you can't make a mess." She bakes these regularly in the five-guestroom farmhouse, built in 1895, that she and husband Christian opened after considerable restoration in 1986.

Another Olympic Lights recipe:
Eggs Olympic, page 97

English Muffin Bread

Ingredients:
2 cups milk or half-and-half
1/2 cup water
Up to 6 cups flour (bread flour preferred)
2 packages active dry yeast, at room temperature
1 tablespoon sugar
2 teaspoons salt
1/4 teaspoon baking soda

Also:
Cornmeal

> In a saucepan, heat milk and water until lukewarm (no higher than 115 degrees).
> In a separate bowl, combine 3 cups flour with yeast, sugar, salt and soda.
> Add milk all at once to flour mixture and beat well. Stir in enough additional flour to make a stiff dough.
> Divide dough into two 9 x 5-inch loaf pans that have been oiled and sprinkled with cornmeal. Sprinkle the top of the dough with cornmeal, as well.
> Cover with a towel, set in a warm place and let rise for at least 1 hour.
> Bake in a preheated oven at 400 degrees for 25 minutes. Remove from the pan immediately.

Makes 2 loaves

from **The Bombay House B&B**
8490 Beck Road NE
Bainbridge Island, WA 98110
206-842-3926

"This bread makes superb toast," said Innkeeper Bunny Cameron, and "it freezes well." She makes it as part of a healthy, hearty breakfast at the five-guestroom B&B she and husband Roger Kanchuck bought in 1986. They were in the process of relocating from Anchorage, and found the 1907 hillside home built by a master shipbuilder, complete with a widow's walk.

Guests reach Bainbridge Island via a beautiful 35-minute ferry ride from downtown Seattle, and the Bombay House is just a short drive from Winslow and dining, golf, clam digging, theater and a marina.

Other Bombay House recipes:
Morning Raspberry Cake, page 28
Citrus Fruit Dip, page 81
Bombay House Granola, page 150

Lemon Huckleberry Bread

Ingredients:

1 cup sugar
1/3 cup butter, softened
3 tablespoons lemon extract
2 eggs
1-1/2 cups sifted flour
1 teaspoon baking powder
1 teaspoon salt
1 cup lemon yogurt
1 cup fresh or frozen (dry pack) huckleberries

Glaze:

1/2 cup sugar
Juice of 1 large lemon
(2-3 tablespoons)

> Line an 8 or 9-inch greased loaf pan with waxed paper. Grease the waxed paper.
> Cream sugar with butter and lemon extract.
> Beat in eggs.
> In a separate bowl, sift together flour, baking powder and salt.
> Add dry ingredients to sugar mixture alternately with yogurt, beating just to blend.
> Fold in huckleberries. Pour into prepared pan.
> Bake in a preheated oven at 350 degrees for 50 to 60 minutes.
> Remove from pan while still warm.
> For Glaze: Combine lemon juice and sugar. Mix well. Brush "glaze" over loaf.
> Best if cut and served cold 24 hours later.

Makes 1 loaf, about 8 servings

from **Mio Amore Pensione**
Little Mountain Road
P.O. Box 208
Trout Lake, WA 98650
509-395-2264

Innkeeper/Pastry Chef Jill Westbrook created this recipe to take advantage of the area's huckleberries, which she says "look very much like a blueberry with a taste between that and a blackberry." Located at 1,800 feet, at the foot of Mt. Adams and in the Gifford Pinchot National Forest, this 1904 farmhouse on the banks of Trout Lake Creek has been transformed into a European-style B&B and a restaurant, where husband/chef Tom specializes in Northern Italian cuisine, by reservation only.

Many of the guests at the four-guestroom B&B have come to sample the food and then, the next day, take advantage of hiking, mountain climbing, white water rafting and walks to waterfalls (plus maybe huckleberry-picking).

Maple Nut Bread

Ingredients:

1 egg
1 cup sugar
1 teaspoon maple flavoring
1 cup milk
1-3/4 cups flour
2 teaspoons baking powder
1/8 teaspoon salt
1 cup walnuts, chopped

> In a large bowl, mix egg, sugar, maple flavoring and milk.
> Sift flour, baking powder and salt together. Then beat into the egg mixture.
> Add chopped walnuts and beat lightly.
> Let this mixture stand in a warm place for 20 minutes.
> Pour into a greased and floured loaf pan.
> Bake in a preheated oven at 325 degrees for 1 hour.

Makes 1 loaf

from **Log Castle B&B**
3273 East Saratoga Road
Langley, WA 98260
206-321-5483

"This was my mother's recipe. It was used when I was a child 60 years ago," notes Innkeeper Norma Metcalf. Norma now serves it at breakfast or along with coffee and tea in the evenings.

Breakfast guests who can tear their eyes away from the magnificent views of Saratoga Passage and the Cascades may notice that the dining room table, made of the end cut of a huge Douglas fir, has a brand, just like brands that tell ownership of cattle. The fir cross-section was a relic from an early log rustler who found broken up log booms after a storm, cut off the branded end of this log and set it afloat, then stole the rest of the log.

This log is just one of many with a story in this three-story log home, hand-built between legislative sessions by State Sen. Jack Metcalf. Jack and Norma opened the four-guestroom B&B in 1986 on a private beach about a mile and a half from the Whidbey Island town of Langley.

Another Log Castle B&B recipe:
Cottage Cheese Hotcakes, page 114

Oregon Hazelnut Sweet Rolls

Ingredients:

4 to 4-1/2 cups flour
1/3 cup sugar
2 teaspoons salt
2 packages active dry yeast
2 teaspoons orange peel, grated
1 cup milk
1/3 cup butter or margarine
2 eggs, slightly beaten

Nut Filling:
1/3 cup butter or margarine,
   softened
1 cup powdered sugar
1 cup hazelnuts, finely
   chopped (use blender)
Glaze:
1/4 cup orange juice
1/4 to 1/2 cup powdered
   sugar

> In a large bowl, combine 2 cups flour, sugar, salt, yeast and orange peel.
> Heat milk and butter until milk is warm (no higher than 115 degrees; butter doesn't need to melt completely).
> Add eggs and warm milk to flour mixture. Blend with an electric mixer at lowest speed until moistened, then beat 3 minutes at medium speed.
> Remove dough from mixer and knead in remaining flour until dough is stiff.
> Cover dough and let rest for 30 minutes.
> Meanwhile, prepare Nut Filling: Mix all ingredients and set aside.
> On a floured board, roll the dough to a 22 x 12-inch rectangle.
> Spread filling over half the dough along the long side. Fold uncovered dough over filling.
> Cut dough crosswise into 1-inch strips. Twist and curl each strip into a round sweet roll shape, tucking the end of the dough underneath.
> Place rolls on greased cookie sheets. Cover and let rise in a warm place until about double in size, about 45 minutes.
> For Glaze: Combine orange juice and sugar.
> Bake rolls in a preheated oven at 350 to 375 degrees for 15-18 minutes, until golden brown. Brush rolls with glaze during the last minutes of baking.

Makes 18-24 rolls

PORTLAND
GUEST HOUSE

from **Portland Guest House**
1720 NE 15th Avenue
Portland, OR 97212
503-282-1402

Innkeeper Susan Gisvold enjoys promoting Oregon's bounty, and this recipe highlights the hazelnut, which she calls one of the state's gems. Susan has lived in this historic neighborhood for nearly 25 years and restored this 100-year-old home as a B&B inn. Guests in her four guestrooms are right around the corner from the popular Holladay Market and the Lloyd Center.

Another Portland Guest House recipe:
Pesto Omelettes, page 102

Sharon's Beachside Banana Bread

Ingredients:

2 cups sugar
1 cup shortening
4 eggs, well beaten
6 ripe bananas
2-1/2 cups flour
1 teaspoon salt
2 teaspoons baking soda

> Cream sugar, shortening, eggs and bananas.
> Sift together dry ingredients. Mix into other ingredients, but do not overmix.
> Grease two bread pans and divide batter between them.
> Bake in a preheated oven at 350 degrees for 55-60 minutes.

Makes 2 loaves

from **Home by the Sea**
2388 East Sunlight Beach Road
Clinton, WA 98236
206-221-2964

Innkeeper Sharon Fritts Drew lived in Iran for six years, teaching health and physical education at Tehran American School. When she left in 1979, "I had to leave everything I owned. This included 20 years of collected recipes." The best of the recipes, however, had been shared with family and friends, and they eventually were returned. That includes this banana bread, which Sharon, and her mother, Helen Fritts, serve at their B&B.

After leaving Iran, Sharon returned "home" to Whidbey Island, to which she had managed to continue coming every summer off while teaching overseas, despite the 10,000 mile commute. She bought property on the beach and decided to open a B&B. After being constructed on Deer Lagoon on Useless Bay, the B&B opened in 1980.

Today, much of the home's decor, such as Persian rugs, reflect her time in the Mid-East. But the home is predominately a beach house, with big driftwood logs coming up to the edge of the patio. Two suites are open, and guests can hot tub on the patio, bring binoculars to watch the birds, or putter their time away on the island's beaches.

Other Home by the Sea recipes:
Pacific Northwest Breakfast Eggs, page 101
Grandma Jenny's Norwegian Brown Cake, page 138
Pears Extraordinaire, page 147

60 Minute Cinnamon Rolls

Ingredients:

3-1/2 to 4-1/2 cups flour
3 tablespoons sugar
1 teaspoon salt
2 packages active dry yeast
1 cup milk
1/2 cup water
1/4 cup margarine

Filling:
  2 tablespoons butter, softened
  1/2 cup sugar
  2 teaspoons cinnamon
"Topping:"
  1/2 cup margarine, melted
  1/2 cup brown sugar, packed
  1/2 cup pecans or walnuts,
      chopped

> Mix 1-1/2 cups flour, sugar, salt and dry yeast in a large bowl.
> Combine milk, water and margarine and heat until very warm (120 degrees).
> Gradually add warm liquid to dry ingredients. With an electric mixer, beat 2 minutes at medium speed, scraping bowl occasionally.
> Add 1/2 cup flour and beat on high speed 2 minutes.
> Stir in enough additional flour to make a soft dough.
> Turn onto board and knead until smooth and elastic, about 5 minutes.
> Place in a greased bowl and turn dough to grease top. Cover and place bowl in a pan of 98-degree water. Let rise 15 minutes. Meanwhile, cover the bottom of a 9 x 13-inch pan with "topping" ingredients.
> Turn out dough onto a floured board and roll into a 10 x 18-inch rectangle.
> Spread with softened butter, then with the mixed sugar and cinnamon.
> Roll dough lengthwise like a jelly roll. Slice off about 18 1-inch slices.
> Place slices, sides touching, evenly over the mixture in the pan in three rows of 6 rolls each. (The rolls can be refrigerated overnight at this point. Remove from the refrigerator and let stand at room temperature the next morning before baking).
> Bake in a preheated oven at 375 degrees for 25 minutes. Invert pan while still warm.

Makes 18 rolls

from **Stange Manor B&B**
1612 Walnut Street
LaGrande, OR 97850
503-963-2400

"On a military base about 15 years ago a friend gave me a recipe for bread or dinner rolls that could be made from start to finish in 60 minutes," said Innkeeper Lynn Hart. "We enjoyed them so much and it was so easy I started making cinnamon rolls the same way." Harts, also restauranteurs, serve these rolls to guests in the 12,000-square-foot mansion they converted to a B&B in 1986. The 1924 Georgian Colonial was built by a lumber baron.

Another Stange Manor recipe:
Savory Baked Eggs, page 103

Strawberry Bread

Ingredients:

3 cups flour
2 cups sugar
1 teaspoon baking soda
1 teaspoon salt
1 tablespoon lemon peel, grated
3 eggs, beaten
1-1/4 cups vegetable oil
2 cups fresh strawberries, cut into chunks

Strawberry Cream Cheese:
6 ounces cream cheese
2 tablespoons strawberry jam

> In a large bowl, mix the flour, sugar, soda, salt and lemon peel.
> In a separate bowl, beat eggs. Stir in oil.
> Stir egg mixture into dry ingredients until moist.
> Fold in berries. Batter should not be too thick. If it appears thick, add a little more oil or juice from berries.
> Pour batter into two greased loaf pans three-quarters full.
> Bake in a preheated oven at 350 degrees for up to 55 minutes.
> Remove from the oven and cool. Loosen with a knife to remove from pans. Serve cool with Strawberry Cream Cheese spread.
> For Strawberry Cream Cheese, soften the cream cheese and mix with jam. Chill until ready to serve.

Makes 2 loaves

from **The White Swan Guest House**
1388 Moore Road
Mount Vernon, WA 98273
206-445-6805

"We have wonderful local produce here," said Innkeeper Peter Goldfarb, so this recipe helps take advantage of the area's strawberries. The bread is served along with fresh fruit to guests in the sunny yellow dining room.

Three guestrooms are available in this restored 1898 Queen Anne farmhouse, complete with white picket fence and English country garden. The B&B is close to the area's renown tulip fields, the towns of LaConner and Mount Vernon and the San Juan Island ferries in Anacortes.

Other White Swan Guest House recipes:
Maple Cream Cheese, page 71
Salmon Spread, page 73
Cherry Scones, page 132
Apple-Oatmeal Crumble, page 142

Whole Wheat Irish Soda Bread

Ingredients:

    3 cups flour
    1 cup whole wheat flour
    1 teaspoon salt
    3 teaspoons baking powder
    1 teaspoon baking soda
    1/4 cup sugar
    1/8 teaspoon cardamom
    1/4 cup butter, at room temperature
    2 cups currants, optional
    1 egg
    1-3/4 cups buttermilk

> Combine the flours, salt, baking powder, soda, sugar and cardamom in a large bowl.
> Cut in the butter with a pastry blender until the mixture is crumbly.
> Add currants.
> In a separate bowl, beat egg with the buttermilk.
> Add egg mixture to the dry ingredients. Stir until blended.
> On a board floured with whole wheat flour, knead dough for 2-3 minutes.
> Divide dough in half. Shape each half into a round loaf.
> Place loaves on a cookie sheet and let them rest for 10 minutes.
> With a sharp knife, cut a cross shape on the tops, slicing approximately a half-inch deep.
> Bake in a preheated oven at 375 degrees for 35-40 minutes.

Makes 2 loaves

from **Salisbury House**
750 16th Avenue E.
Seattle, WA 98112
206-328-8682

This bread got Innkeeper Cathryn Wiese out of a pinch. "I made this recipe one day for some visitors from the Seattle Convention and Visitors Bureau and realized at the last moment I was almost out of flour. So I substituted the whole wheat flour, and we were all delighted with the extra crunch it gave the soda bread." At Salisbury House, visitors are served the bread warm with homemade strawberry and raspberry preserves. Cathryn and Mary Wiese pick berries on summer afternoons at the region's "U-pick" farms.

Other Salisbury House recipes:
Ginger Pear Muffins, page 40
South of the Border Quiche, page 105
Mary's Citrus French Toast, page 108

Why settle for "just plain" maple syrup on your pancakes, cream cheese on your bagels or butter on your bran muffins? Instead, serve a warm Cinnamon Cream Syrup over pancakes, waffles or French toast. Try Salmon Spread on bagels. Maple Cream Cheese or Zest Butter make "health food" bran muffins enjoyable. And perish the thought of stirring up hollandaise sauce from a foil packet mix ever again (the homemade stuff is unforgettable). There's even a recipe for fruit-filled Naturally Sweet Fruit Syrup and one for Festive Marmalade to brighten any table.

Preserves, Butters, Spreads & Sauces

Cinnamon Cream Syrup

Ingredients:

    1/2 cup butter, melted
    1 cup heavy cream
    1 teaspoon cinnamon
    1/4 teaspoon allspice
    3 to 4 tablespoons sugar

> Combine all ingredients in a saucepan.
> Stir over medium heat until all ingredients have combined and are hot.
> Serve warm over French toast or apple pancakes.

Makes 8 servings

from **Chambered Nautilus**
5005 22nd Avenue NE
Seattle, WA 98105
206-522-2536

"This seems to work very well on a variety of things and also will keep about a week in the icebox," said Innkeeper Bunny Hagemeyer. She likes to use it in the winter instead of fresh fruit syrups, when the cinnamon scent and flavor are especially inviting.

This Georgian Colonial home has been open as a B&B inn since 1983, but Bunny and Bill have been offering their special hospitality since they purchased it in 1988. Guests have their choice of six large rooms, four with porches, and two with dormered windows on the quiet third floor. The home was built in 1915 by Annie Kay and Dr. Herbert Gowen, who founded the Department of Oriental Studies at the University of Washington, just a few blocks away. There have been four subsequent owners, one of whom hand-painted blue flowers on the wallpaper in one of the guestrooms.

Bunny and Bill entered innkeeping after successful corporate careers. Breakfast here is served in the dining room, and on cool days, a fire is lit in the fireplace. The menu varies, but the food always is acccompanied by background chamber music and cups of dark-roasted Italian blend coffee. Guests are fortified for a day downtown, just 10 minutes away, at the University, within walking distance, or playing in the Greenlake or Ravenna parks or on the Burke-Gilman bike trail.

Other Chambered Nautilus recipes:
Apple Quiche, page 87
Blueberry Serenescene, page 125

Homemade Hollandaise

Ingredients:

    3 egg yolks OR 1 whole egg and 2 yolks
    Juice of 1/2 lemon (1-2 tablespoons)
    1/8 teaspoon Dijon mustard
    1/4 cup butter, melted

> Place egg yolks in blender.
> Turn on blender and add lemon juice.
> Add mustard.
> Turn blender on low. Drizzle in melted butter.
> Pour the mixture into a pitcher (or top of double boiler) and keep it warm over simmering water ("Not too hot or mixture will become lumpy!").

Makes 1 cup

from **The Gallery B&B at Little Cape Horn**
4 Little Cape Horn
Cathlamet, WA 98612
206-425-7395

Hollandaise sauce, so rich and creamy, is easier to make than one might think, says Innkeeper Carolyn Feasey, who regularly makes it as part of her Eggs Benedict in Puff Pastry entree.

Carolyn and husband Eric enjoy sharing their in-the-heart-of-it-all contemporary home with B&B guests. They opened two guestrooms in 1985 and now have four rooms to rent. The home faces the Columbia River, and tugboats and ships, eagles and herons, hummingbirds and hawks are often coming and going. The home is just four miles east of Cathlamet, and the area draws windsurfers, beachcombers, stargazers and nature lovers.

"When the local hotel closed in the 1980s there was only one room available to rent in our entire county," said Carolyn. "So we decided that we would open our extra bedrooms." Carolyn and Eric raised "two daughters, a Labrador retriever and many cats" at this home.

Other Gallery B&B recipes:
Banana Mango Loaf, page 55
Eggs Benedict in Puff Pastry, page 94

Festive Marmalade

Ingredients:

16 ounces of homemade or favorite orange marmalade
1 tablespoon lemon juice, freshly-squeezed
1/3 cup walnuts, coarsely chopped
12 to 15 maraschino cherries, drained and chopped
1/3 cup golden raisins

> In a large bowl, combine all ingredients. Mix well.
> Store in a covered dish with a tight-fitting lid.
> Keep refrigerated.

Makes 2-1/2 cups

from **Cedarym**
1011 240th Avenue NE
Redmond, WA 98053
206-868-4159

"We needed a rather festive spread for our bran muffins served at a special family dinner many years ago," said Innkeeper Mary Ellen Brown. "This marmalade became that special spread. The cherries, nuts and raisins really dress up a simple marmalade."

Since 1984, she and Walt have been serving this for breakfast on muffins and in their filled French toast, called "Surprise French Toast." The Browns had built their retirement home on 2.5 beautiful, secluded acres in Redmond. But they wanted more than hobbies to keep busy and turned to the hospitality business of innkeeping.

Innkeeping also allowed them to share their home with others. They built it as a replica of an historic New England Colonial, complete with a walk-in fireplace hearth in the "keeping" (family) room, an antique door knocker, a "caged onion" lamp on the post and a colonial flag outside with only 13 stars. Mary Ellen dips her own candles and breakfast is served by candlelight, though she prepares it in a modern kitchen. The two guestrooms are upstairs, with antique brass beds and hand-stencilled borders, completed by Walt. To reach the rooms, guests climb up a stairway, made with a steeper pitch to be authentic for the period.

Other Cedarym recipes:
Surprise French Toast, page 111
Christmas Stollen, page 134
Cedarym Oats, page 151

Maple Cream Cheese

Ingredients:

3 ounces cream cheese, softened
2 tablespoons pure maple syrup

> Mix ingredients and put in a small dish or crock. Chill. Serve with hot muffins or cold breads.

Makes about 4 servings

from **The White Swan Guest House**
1388 Moore Road
Mount Vernon, WA 98273
206-445-6805

"This is great on banana bread or bran muffins," said Innkeeper Peter Goldfarb. The recipe is so simple even busy innkeepers like himself can stir it up on rushed mornings, though it's probably best a day or two later, when the maple flavor has had a chance to pervade the cream cheese.

Peter, a transplanted Manhattanite and interior designer/contractor, found this 1898 farmhouse while exploring the Skagit Valley in 1986. He undertook restoration himself, using historic photos as guides.

"This old house was built in 1898 by a Scandinavian farmer and fell into disrepair in the '40s," Peter said. "By the time I found it, it had had some work done on it, but needed new plumbing and just about everything *but* a new roof." To say he redid it from "the ground up" is accurate. The house literally was sinking into the fertile farmland, so the first project was to lift it, remove the old foundation and put in a new one.

Three-and-a-half years later, Peter's got the place redone, added an old-fashioned back porch, and replenished the gardens with new fruit trees, berry bushes and plenty of flowers. A "honeymoon cabin" also is finished.

It's no wonder Peter was captivated by the area and decided to settle here. In the spring, when the area's tulip fields are in full bloom, travelers come from afar to get a glimpse. Photos of the fields are recognized the world over and rival those of the Netherlands.

Other White Swan Guest House recipes:
Strawberry Bread, page 65
Salmon Spread, page 73
Cherry Scones, page 132
Apple-Oatmeal Crumble, page 142

Naturally Sweet Fruit Syrup

Ingredients:

1 12-ounce can frozen unsweetened apple juice
3 tablespoons arrowroot flour or powder
4 cups favorite berries or cut-up fruit ("Our favorite fruits to use are
blueberries and strawberries.")

> Thaw the apple juice and empty it into a large saucepan.
> Mix in the arrowroot flour with a wire whisk.
> Heat over medium flame, stirring constantly.
> Before the mixture thickens, add the berries or fruit.
> Continue to heat and stir until thickened. Serve hot over pancakes, waffles or French toast.

Makes 8 servings

from **Spring Creek Llama Ranch**
14700 NE Spring Creek Lane
Newberg, OR 97132
503-538-5717

There's nothing wrong with "all natural" maple syrup, but this recipe gave Innkeeper Melinda Van Bossuyt the chance to use fresh Oregon fruit and stay away from syrups which are full of corn syrup or other sweeteners.

Melinda and husband Dave promise a warm welcome at their large home, but not as warm as the welcome guests receive outside from the resident llamas, who greet them with a llama kiss. Clearly, Van Bossuyts are two of a growing number of ranchers who are hooked on these beasts. "We moved to this wonderful setting from a place on top of the mountain about a mile from here," Melinda explains. "We wanted more land for raising llamas and decided that this enormous house with its five bedrooms and four bathrooms would work well as a bed and breakfast." They opened two guestrooms in 1989 and also take in traveling llamas for "barn & breakfast."

"We breed and raise them to sell as pets and packers," Melinda said about the llamas, some of which she calls "our boys." "Also, we harvest the wool and market it to handspinners." Guests find themselves in the middle of 24 acres of forest and pasture and next door to two wineries, Rex Hill and Veritas.

Other Spring Creek Llama Ranch recipes:
Melinda's Whole Wheat Blueberry Muffins, page 43
Melinda's Famous Wholegrain Waffles, page 122
Our Favorite Oatmeal-Raisin Cookie, page 160

Salmon Spread

Ingredients:

6 ounces cream cheese, softened
2 tablespoons milk or sour cream
1 tablespoon chives, chopped
1/2 cup smoked salmon, flaked
1/2 to 1 teaspoon white horseradish, optional

> Mix all ingredients thoroughly.
> Spoon into a crock and chill. Best when made a day ahead.
> Serve on toasted thin-sliced or mini bagels or on crackers.

Makes about 6 servings

from **The White Swan Guest House**
1388 Moore Road
Mount Vernon, WA 98273
206-445-6805

Innkeeper Peter Goldfarb leaves out the horseradish for breakfast guests, since it'd be a bit overpowering the first thing in the morning. But he enjoys the tang when the recipe is served as an evening snack to spread on crackers. His smoked salmon may have come from the Pacific Northwest Indian Smoked Salmon company of the Swinomish Indian reservation, which operates just over the scenic bridge in LaConner.

It seems guests rarely are around much in the evenings because they, like Peter, have been captivated by the area. They are off taking bike rides on back roads, bird watching, or walking along the Skagit River, which runs right in front of the house. In April, of course, they are gawking at the millions of tulip and daffodil blooms in fields a stone's throw from the house. If it's too rainy or cold to be outdoors, guests may enjoy warm restaurants, galleries, antique and gift shops in LaConner, just six miles away. They come home to a hot woodstove in the parlor and homemade cookies.

Peter has three guestrooms in this 1898 farmhouse, completely restored and decorated with antiques, plus a private guest cottage in the gardens.

Other White Swan Guest House recipes:
Strawberry Bread, page 65
Maple Cream Cheese, page 71
Cherry Scones, page 132
Apple-Oatmeal Crumble, page 142

Zest Butter

Ingredients:

Zest (peel) from 1 orange, finely grated
1/2 cup orange juice
1-1/4 cups butter
8 ounces cream cheese
1-1/4 cups powdered sugar

> Place the freshly-grated orange peel and juice in a small saucepan. Simmer until the amount of liquid is reduced by one-half. Remove from heat and cool.
> In a separate bowl, cream the butter and cream cheese until fluffy.
> Add powdered sugar alternately with juice until the mixture reaches a nice, spreadable consistency.
> Chill to thicken. Store in the refrigerator or freezer.
> If desired, spoon the softened mixture into butter molds and freeze, then remove individual molds as needed.

Makes 4 cups

from **DeCann House B&B**
2610 Eldridge Avenue
Bellingham, WA 98225
206-734-9172

Innkeeper Barbara Hudson keeps the frozen butter molds full of this sweet butter, then takes out enough molds for breakfast. Guests enjoy it on hot muffins and pancakes. "This recipe came from a friend, specifically for the B&B," she said. "I have experimented with softening the butter in the microwave to cream with the cream cheese more evenly."

Breakfasts aren't the only thing homemade in this B&B, which she and Van opened in 1986. In addition to teaching, both have other skills. Van is an old-home lover and woodworker. He has built the "grandmother" clock and bed frames, for instance. Barbara is a glass hobbyist who has her works throughout the house.

The DeCann House, built at the turn of the century, overlooks Bellingham Bay. Bellingham is also the home of Western Washington University.

Another DeCann House recipe:
Amazing Strawberries, page 76

One of the true benefits of living in or visiting the Pacific Northwest is its fabulous abundance of fresh fruit. While many innkeepers have devised muffin, bread or entree recipes simply to use up the over-supply from their pear or plum trees or berry patches, many offer a fruit dish as a special side dish. Even if we can't pick our own fruit, the natural sweetness of fruit is a wonderful way to start the day. In cold weather, as these recipes show, there's no reason to give up the fruit — just turn up the heat and bake or broil it!

Fruits

Amazing Strawberries

Ingredients:
　　2 cups orange juice
　　1/4 to 1/2 cup sugar
　　1/2 cup sherry
　　1 quart (4 cups) fresh strawberries, sliced or halved
Also:
　　Powdered sugar

> Combine orange juice and sugar.
> Cook on high in microwave 3-4 minutes to dissolve sugar. Then cool bowl in refrigerator.
> Stir in sherry.
> Pour over berries until covered. Marinate in the refrigerator overnight.
> Sprinkle with powdered sugar and serve in fruit bowls.

Makes 4 servings

from **DeCann House B&B**
2610 Eldridge Avenue
Bellingham, WA 98225
206-734-9172

"The fresh strawberries and sherry combine to create the most delicious tangy tartness," said Innkeeper Barbara Hudson, who created this recipe based on suggestions for fresh fruit marinades. "We serve this with warm muffins and encourage guests to drink the nectar to the last drop." Fresh Washington strawberries are heavenly during June, but Barbara admits that "we hedge on the season and use out-of-area berries sometimes."

Barbara and husband Van opened this turn-of-the-century home as a two-guestroom B&B in 1986. They are teachers and lifelong Pacific Northwest residents who have traveled throughout this country, Europe and the Caribbean. "Our bed and breakfast tries to combine the intimacy of European hospitality with the convenience American travelers are used to," she said. That includes the hosts gladly spending time with guests to talk about the home's renovation, history and family heirlooms furnishing it. They also are particularly eager to talk about beautiful Bellingham, halfway between Seattle and Vancouver at the top of Puget Sound.

Another DeCann House recipe:
Zest Butter, page 74

Baked Apples

Ingredients:
4 crisp apples (Granny Smith preferred), washed and cored
2 tablespoons raisins
2 tablespoons wheat germ
1 tablespoon walnuts, chopped
2 tablespoons brown sugar, packed

Also:
Butter
Maple syrup
Cream, half-and-half or milk

> Mix raisins, wheat germ, walnuts and brown sugar.
> Fill cavities of the apples with the mixture.
> Dot tops of apples with butter.
> Drizzle with maple syrup.
> Place in a baking dish containing one cup boiling water.
> Bake in a preheated oven at 375 degrees for 45 minutes or until tender, basting with pan juices.
> Serve in individual bowls with pan juices. Pass the cream, half-and-half or milk.

Makes 4 servings

from **Mt. Ashland Inn**
550 Mt. Ashland Road
Ashland, OR 97520
503-482-8707

These hot baked apples are a wonderful addition to a winter breakfast, when guests by the huge dining room window can see the snow hanging in the trees. Innkeeper Elaine Shanafelt is a nurse, and she has adapted this recipe, as she does most, for reduced fats and increased fiber.

Elaine and Jerry began this 4,200-square-foot log home on their 160 acres in 1985, designing it specifically as a B&B. More than 275 cedar logs were cut on the property for the house. Jerry is a designer and builder and he did much of the work, down to the stained glass. Elaine and Jerry and their two Alaskan huskies, which are former members of their sled dog teams, have welcomed guests to the four-guestroom inn since early 1988.

Another Mt. Ashland Inn recipe:
Apple Bundt Cake, page 24

Baked Grapefruit

Ingredients:
   2 grapefruit
   4 teaspoons berry jam (strawberry, huckleberry or raspberry suggested)
Also:
   1/2 cup or so fresh berries

> Cut each grapefruit in half.
> Loosen each section with a sharp knife.
> Top halves with 1 teaspoon each berry jam.
> Microwave at high for 2 minutes. Rotate and microwave again for 2 to 3 minutes, or until grapefruit are hot and juicy.
> Top each half with fresh berries and serve.

Makes 4 servings

from **Syndicate Hill B&B**
403 South Sixth Street
Dayton, WA 99328
509-382-2688

"This is really pretty and is great on a cool morning," said Innkeeper Sandy Conlee. Sandy, who uses jams made from local berries, has been making this grapefruit for guests since she and husband Len opened their B&B in 1988. "Try pears or peaches, too," she said. "They are great served with a dab of jam and heated in the microwave."

This home's builder originally purchased the land for $50 in 1902 from the Syndicate Hill Land Company. The home was built five years later and has been owned by a few successful Eastern Washington businessmen. Sandy, a computer operator, and Len, a utility lineman, purchased the Queen Anne Victorian in 1983 when they moved to Dayton from Corvallis, Ore.

When they discovered the large home was really bigger than they needed, Conlees took a friend's suggestion and converted it into the county's first B&B. They made several improvements before opening, and spent countless hours doing research and seeking county and city approval. Today, Syndicate Hill B&B has two upstairs guestrooms and an outdoor hot tub. Guests also are welcome to use the family room and TV.

The B&B is within walking distance of the historic downtown, restaurants, an historic walking tour, museum, art gallery and antique shops. It's close to fishing, boating and waterskiing on the Snake River and berry picking, hiking, hunting and skiing in the Blue Mountains.

Breakfast Parfait

Ingredients:
    1 cup assorted fruits and berries
    1/4 cup granola
    1/2 to 3/4 cup vanilla or pina colada yogurt
Also:
    Additional granola
    Slices of fruit

> Mix all ingredients, or layer fruit, granola and yogurt in parfait glasses, ending with yogurt on top.
> Sprinkle the top with granola and place a slice of fruit on top.
> Serve right away or chill.

Makes 2 servings

from **The Blackberry Inn**
Highway 101
P.O. Box 188
Seal Rock, OR 97367
503-563-2259

"This is a breakfast in itself, but we serve it as a first course," said Innkeeper Barbara Tarter. "Although it contains 'the dreaded yogurt,' our guests think it is good to the very last drop." Barbara uses blackberries (of course), strawberries, bananas, blueberries, peaches, grapes, melon or a combination, adding fruit cocktail if some of these are not available.

Barbara has modeled her B&B after those in Europe. "In 1983, I visited Great Britain for three weeks," Barbara said. "I was dissatisfied with hotels, so reluctantly I tried a B&B — I didn't want to stay in a stranger's house — and was hooked." Blackberry Inn opened in the small home in 1985.

Guests have a private entrance and parlor and may use the whirlpool on the deck. Breakfast is served in the kitchen near the antique wood stove. It often includes egg dishes from the red hens and blackberry jam from the canes on Barbara's property.

Seal Rock is attractive to beachcombers, who can explore tidepools, rock formations, go clamming, whale watch or go crabbing at Alsea Bay.

Another Blackberry Inn recipe:
Apple Cream Cheese Omelette, page 86

Caitlin's Cottage Cheese Fruit Delight

Ingredients:

    3 cups low-fat cottage cheese
    1/4 cup sugar
    1/2 teaspoon vanilla
    1 teaspoon lemon peel, freshly grated
    1/2 teaspoon lemon juice
    3 cups mixed fresh fruit — strawberries, raspberries, blueberries, pitted cherries,
        loganberries, marion berries, peaches, watermelon, cantaloupe and honey dew
        melon are favorites

> In the blender, blend cottage cheese, sugar, vanilla, lemon peel and lemon juice until smooth.
> Refrigerate blended ingredients until ready to serve.
> In individual compote dishes, alternate layers of cottage cheese mixture and fruit, ending with fruit on top.
> Serve immediately or refrigerate again.
> Variation: "This also may be served as a breakfast pie by layering the cottage cheese mix, followed by a layer of fruit, on top of a graham cracker crust."

Makes 8 servings

from **Littlefield House**
401 North Howard Street
Newberg, OR 97132
503-538-9868

"We are very fortunate to live in the Willamette Valley and in Yamhill County where fresh fruits are so plentiful and delicious," said Innkeeper Elizabeth Teitzel. "Our daughter Caitlin, 12, who loves fresh fruits more than candy, was my taste critic for this recipe. She says the fruit needs to be the main taste 'event' in the dish, so we don't use as much sugar as some people might like." Elizabeth encourages experimenting with the cottage cheese mixture.

Elizabeth and Bert serve this dish often from May through August when various fruits are at their peak. Breakfast is in the dining room in this spacious 1909 home, which Dr. Horace Littlefield had constructed for his wife, Maggie. The natural woodwork, beveled leaded glass and other features showing the original craftsmanship still remain. Downtown is a short walk.

Other Littlefield House recipes:
Aunt Pete's Wild Blueberry Muffins, page 34
Bert's Bran Muffins, page 36
Elizabeth's Broiled Breakfast Sticks, page 82

Citrus Fruit Dip

Ingredients:

1 14-ounce can sweetened condensed milk
1/2 cup orange juice concentrate, thawed
1/2 cup water
2 tablespoons orange rind or fresh rind from two oranges, grated
3-6 cups assorted fresh fruit, sliced

> In a small bowl, combine condensed milk, juice concentrate, water and orange rind.
> Chill overnight to blend flavors. Keep refrigerated until ready to use.
> Place the dip in a small glass bowl in the center of a large platter. Arrange fresh, sliced fruit around the dip. Complementary fresh fruit includes any kind of melon, pineapple, seedless grapes and strawberries. Blueberries, raspberries, star fruit or kiwi, though hard to dip, make beautiful garnishes.
> Guests may use toothpicks to dip the fruit.

Makes 2-1/2 cups dip

from **The Bombay House B&B**
8490 Beck Road NE
Bainbridge Island, WA 98110
206-842-3926

"This citrus dip is also a great dressing for a fruit salad," said Innkeeper Bunny Cameron. She developed the recipe for her catering company in Anchorage, which specialized in hors d'oeuvres and finger food. "The dip will keep refrigerated for about two weeks." Those who enjoy granola can stir or layer granola and fruit into a Citrus Fruit Dip parfait.

Bunny and husband Roger Kanchuk serve this to guests who find fresh Washington fruit a real treat. Homemade muffins, coffeecakes and breads are set out each morning for a family-style buffet. The home is located in the former "mill town" of West Blakely, home to the largest lumber mill in the world in the mid 1800s, and now what Bunny says is "a sleepy, unincorporated community." Bainbridge Island is a haven just a 35-minute ferry ride from downtown Seattle. Bunny and Roger purchased this 1907 home in 1986, and have five guestrooms for folks who want to get away without going too far. The island has back roads to explore, beaches to comb and to dig clams, and there is fine dining, as well.

Other Bombay House recipes:
Morning Raspberry Cake, page 28
English Muffin Bread, page 59
Bombay House Granola, page 150

Elizabeth's Broiled Breakfast Sticks

Ingredients:

    1 20-ounce can pineapple chunks, drained
    24 small to medium fresh mushrooms
    1 large apple (Granny Smith, Newton or other tart cooking apple preferred)
    1/2 cup butter or margarine, melted
    1/2 cup maple syrup, warmed

> Drain pineapple.
> Cut stems off mushrooms and wash thoroughly.
> Quarter apple, remove core. Cut quarters in half lengthwise to make eight sections. Then cut sections into thirds.
> Place ingredients alternately on a kabob stick.
> Brush with melted butter and then with maple syrup.
> Broil for 4-5 minutes on each side.
> Serve immediately with eggs and hot biscuits or muffins.
> Variation: Include pre-cooked ham chunks or sausage links cut in thirds.

Makes 8 servings

from **Littlefield House**
401 North Howard Street
Newberg, OR 97132
503-538-9868

"This is one of my favorites — it combines some very nice flavors and textures," said Innkeeper Elizabeth Teitzel. "I like to serve this as a vegetarian dish. It is a nice change from cereals and fruit." Either with or without meat, "this always gets positive reviews" from guests.

Elizabeth and Bert found the interior of their large 1909 home in Newberg in nearly original condition. Inside is natural woodwork and leaded, beveled glass, some of the features that Dr. Horace Littlefield insisted upon when he had the home built for Maggie, his wife.

Guests at the Littlefield House are made to feel at home by Teitzels, who enjoy sharing their home with others. Wine-tasting tours of the Yamhill County vineyards, antiquing and picnicking are among choices for a getaway.

Other Littlefield House recipes:
Aunt Pete's Wild Blueberry Muffins, page 34
Bert's Bran Muffins, page 36
Caitlin's Cottage Cheese Fruit Delight, page 80

Hawaiian Bananas

Ingredients:

Bananas, ripe but very firm
Sour cream
Lemon juice
Coconut, shredded

> Peel and slice the bananas into 1/2 to 3/4-inch pieces.
> Dip into the lemon juice, then into the sour cream (coat well).
> Roll in the coconut until well coated.
> Place in a covered container and chill thoroughly.

from **The Handmaiden's Inn**
230 Red Spur Drive
Grants Pass, OR 97527
503-476-2932

"This is a recipe we used a lot for garnishing in our catering business," said Bette Hammer, who, with daughter Jody, owned a catering service in Palos Verdes, Calif. "It is a beautiful accompaniment for a fruit plate or as an after-breakfast treat."

Since 1985, Bette and Jody have been catering to B&B guests in their three-guestroom inn, the purchase of which spurred the move to Oregon. With Bette's 20 years teaching home economics, Jody's experience as a microwave cooking instructor, and their combined catering experience, guests are delighted with breakfasts here. In addition, home-made dinners and picnic hampers for hikers or day-trippers can be arranged. Other touches, like homemade truffles on the nightstand, make guests feel pampered.

Located five miles outside of Grants Pass, their new three-story cedar home has views of the Rogue River Valley. While the home is modern, it is decorated with "country" touches. One guestroom has a vaulted cedar ceiling; another has an old-fashioned iron-and-brass bed.

Guests often awaken to the smell of Kahlua Fudge coffee brewing, which arrives at their door along with the morning paper. Jody and Bette report enjoying a considerably slower pace than their California catering business allowed, but they remain busy. Bette took on the task of organizing and distributing Oregon's first B&B directory, giving travelers a listing of B&Bs they can contact directly.

Peach Kuchen

Ingredients:

1 16-ounce can peach halves
1-1/2 cups flour
1/2 cup sugar
2 teaspoons baking powder
1 teaspoon orange peel, grated
1/2 teaspoon salt
2 eggs, beaten
1/4 cup butter, melted

Topping:
1/2 teaspoon cinnamon
2 tablespoons sugar
1/4 teaspoon nutmeg

> Drain peaches, saving 2 tablespoons of the "juice."
> Combine flour, sugar, baking powder, orange peel and salt.
> In a separate bowl, beat eggs and combine with the reserved peach juice and melted butter.
> Pour egg mixture into the dry ingredients and blend, but don't overmix.
> Spread batter in the bottom of a greased 8-1/2 inch quiche pan, springform pan or tart pan with a removable sides/bottom.
> Top with peach halves, cut side down.
> Mix the topping ingredients. Sprinkle the mixture over peach halves.
> Bake in a preheated oven at 400 degrees for 25 minutes. Cool 10 minutes before serving. Place pan on a serving plate, then remove the sides.

Makes 6 servings

from **The Gilbert Inn**
341 Beach Drive
Seaside, OR 97138
503-738-9770

"This goes great with egg dishes and is great when served warm," said Innkeeper Carole Rees, who was given the recipe by a guest of the inn. Carole and Dick serve breakfast in the sun room of this 1892 Queen Anne Victorian mansion, formerly the home of Alexander Gilbert, one of Seaside's founders and prominent residents.

This is Dick and Carole's second inn in Seaside, where they admittedly are hooked on the shops, restaurants and beaches. The Gilbert Inn is located one block from the historic promenade walk along the ocean. The 10 guestrooms in this home are furnished mostly in a country French decor and antiques. Downstairs, the big parlor fireplace is a popular gathering spot, and guests marvel at the natural fir tongue-and-groove ceilings and walls throughout Gilbert's proud home.

As might be expected at these B&B inns, amazing things are done daily with the ordinary, inexpensive, always-on-hand egg. From apples, artichokes and avacados to ripe olives, smoked salmon and spinach, the combinations are marvelous. Likewise, innkeepers have a way of making elegant creations out of what used to be rather mundane French toast, pancakes or waffles. Then there are some entrees that defy categorizing, including a whole salmon cooked by a crusty sea captain. The secrets of those super-special B&B brunches are secrets no more!

Entrees

Apple Cream Cheese Omelette

Ingredients:
2 tablespoons butter
1/4 cup sugar
1 teaspoon cinnamon
Juice of 1/2 lemon (1-2 tablespoons)
2 medium apples (Golden Delicious preferred), peeled and thinly sliced
1 tablespoon almond-flavored liqueur, optional
10 eggs, beaten
3 ounces cream cheese, cut into four long pieces

> Melt butter in a frying pan. Stir in sugar, cinnamon and lemon juice.
> Add apples and saute just until tender.
> Stir in liqueur, then keep mixture warm.
> Pour one-quarter of the eggs into a heated, 10-inch omelette pan. Twirl gently to cook egg, then turn over (do not overcook).
> In the center of the omelette, place one-quarter of the apple mixture and a piece of the cream cheese.
> Roll edges of the omelette to the center. Turn it upside down onto a serving plate.
> Repeat for three more omelettes.

Makes 4 servings

from **The Blackberry Inn**
Highway 101
P.O. Box 188
Seal Rock, OR 97367
503-563-2259

"Our little red hens take such good care of us that I needed a recipe to take care of the extra eggs," said Innkeeper Barbara Tarter. "After experimenting on my family, I began serving this apple-filled omelette to our guests." Breakfast begins with a breakfast fruit parfait and continues with bran muffins, maple sausage and these omelettes.

For Barbara, operating her own B&B is something like child's play. "I started cooking young and always loved tea parties with my dolls, so this business is a continuation of my favorite childhood play." Three guestrooms were opened in her home in 1985.

Another Blackberry Inn recipe:
Breakfast Parfait, page 79

Apple Quiche

Ingredients:

1 deep dish 8-inch OR 1 regular 9-inch pie shell
3 cooking apples (Granny Smith preferred), peeled, cored and thinly sliced
1/2 cup light brown sugar, lightly packed
2 teaspoons cinnamon
1 cup heavy cream
2 or 3 eggs, beaten
8 ounces monterey jack cheese, shredded

> Prebake pie shell in a preheated oven at 400 degrees until lightly browned. Leave oven on.
> Heap apples into the pie shell. Sprinkle with brown sugar and cinnamon.
> In a separate bowl, beat the cream into the eggs. (Do not beat so long that cream whips.)
> Pour egg mixture over apples and top with shredded cheese. Make sure all apples are covered with cheese, so pat it into place, if necessary.
> Bake at 400 degrees for 1 hour until apples are tender and custard is set.
> Remove from oven and let quiche sit for about 10 minutes before serving on warm plates.

Makes 5-6 servings

from **Chambered Nautilus**
5005 22nd Avenue NE
Seattle, WA 98105
206-522-2536

"This recipe was devised to use at our Sunday morning buffet," explains Innkeeper Bunny Hagemeyer. "The quiche is also a way for us to tell our guests about the noble apple, one of Washington's finest crops." Bunny, who once took cooking classes taught by James Beard and who got lots of practice while raising eight children, now puts her talent to good use at the inn.

"My husband, Bill, and I decided a few years ago that we would like to leave corporate life," said Bunny. She and Bill bought this Seattle inn in 1988, five years after it opened. Bill had an advertising and public relations background, and Bunny had an operations management background, both necessary in innkeeping. They also brought considerable hospitality skills.

The Chambered Nautilus has six guestrooms in a large 1915 Georgian Colonial home. Perched on a hill near the University of Washington, the B&B is an easy walk from the University and downtown is a 10-minute drive.

Other Chambered Nautilus recipes:
Cinnamon Cream Syrup, page 68
Blueberry Serenescene, page 125

Asparagus Herb Cheese Omelettes

Ingredients:

    1/2 pound fresh asparagus spears, cut into 2-3 inch pieces
    1/4 pound low-salt bacon
    1/4 cup plain (unmarinated) artichoke hearts, quartered
    8 eggs, slightly beaten
    Herb cheese (such as Alouette or other brands, or make your own with cream cheese,
        garlic and fresh herbs)

Also:

    Cream cheese
    Fresh herbs and/or green pepper, chopped

> Steam aspargus just until crunchy. Do not overcook.
> Cook bacon until crisp. Drain and crumble.
> Warm artichoke hearts in a microwave or oven.
> Prepare good omelette pans and add the eggs, two per omelette.
> On half of the omelette, add a handful of warm asparagus pieces, two artichoke heart quarters, 2-3 tablespoons of bacon pieces, and 2-3 tablespoons herb cheese. (If the cheese is either strong or salty, add a dab of plain cream cheese.)
> Place unrolled omelette under broiler for 20 seconds to further melt cheese and blend ingredients.
> Remove from broiler, fold and place on a warm plate. Garnish with herbs and green pepper and serve immediately.

Makes 4 servings

from **The Inn at Swifts Bay**
Port Stanley Road
Route 2, Box 3402
Lopez Island, WA 98261
206-468-3636

"This recipe was developed since there is an abundance of fresh asparagus from the Skagit Valley and other areas during the spring," said Innkeeper Chris Brandmeir. "The artichoke adds tartness and the herb cheese a nice flavor, without overpowering the fresh asparagus."

Chris and Robert Herrmann opened this four-guestroom inn in the spring of 1988. The contemporary Tudor home has an outdoor whirlpool hot tub and, in the living room and den, a well-used fireplace, which welcomes guests back after a day of whale watching, beachcombing or bike riding.

Other Inn at Swifts Bay recipes:
Eggs Dungeness, page 95
Inn at Swifts Bay Potatoes, page 159

Captain Pedro's Private Stores

Ingredients:
1 ripe avocado
2 "almost cooked" poached eggs
2 "slabs of cheese" (sharp cheddar preferred)
2 tablespoons hot salsa
Pinch of Johnny's Salad Elegance
Also:
Ripe olives
Dried seaweed, optional

> Slice the avocado in half and remove the pit.
> Into each half, place an almost-cooked egg.
> Cover with a slice of cheese, "on top of which dump salsa."
> Bake in a preheated oven at 400 degrees for "plus or minus" 8 minutes.
> "After baking melts the cheese and finishes getting the egg cooked, serve in a shallow dish.
Top with a pinch or shake or two of Salad Elegance." Garnish with olives and seaweed.

Makes 2 servings

KRESTINE
1904

from **Tall Ship Ketch Krestine**
3311 Harborview Drive
Gig Harbor, WA 98335
206-858-9395

"In three-and-a-half years, this dish has never been returned to the galley!" notes Capt. Pedro himself, a.k.a. Peter Darrah, who claims to offer "Hammock and Hardtack on Tall Ship," but about whom we get the feeling we better not take literally, or seriously, even: "My cooking expertise stems from a merit badge earned in the Boy Scouts. No improvement since then."

"Capt. Pete" opened his 1904 100-foot coastal sailing trader, moored in Gig Harbor, as a B&B in 1986. But he's been eating this dish since he was a little boy. "When my mother was born, my grandparents were stationed in Zamboanga, Philippine Islands. The gist of this recipe came from a Spanish house servant named Victoria. Both my grandmother, Irma, and my mother, Marjorie, would fix this for Sunday morning." The credit for the pinch of "Johnny's Salad Elegance" goes to the Captain alone.

Guests sleep in the stateroom or two smaller cabins and dine in the saloon on WWII surplus U.S. Navy china and flatware. "The atmosphere is enhanced by the use of oil lamps, lots of old nautical stuff all over the place, and no TV."

Another Tall Ship Ketch Krestine recipe:
Sea Bag Salmon, page 128

Celebration Eggs

Ingredients:

    1 cup fresh mushrooms, sliced (optional)
    6 tablespoons butter
    6 tablespoons flour
    3-1/2 cups half-and-half
    2 cups chicken broth
    1/2 cup dry sherry
    1 to 1-1/2 cups cooked shrimp
    3 cups plain (unmarinated) artichoke hearts, drained and quartered
    24 eggs
    12 tablespoons butter, melted
    1-1/2 cups monterey jack cheese, grated

> Saute mushrooms and set aside.
> Melt butter in a large skillet. Stir in flour and cook until bubbly.
> Gradually stir in half-and-half, chicken broth and sherry until sauce is thick and smooth.
> Gently stir in shrimp, artichoke hearts and mushrooms.
> At this point, sauce can be refrigerated overnight.
> Butter 12 ramekins or individual au gratin dishes. Spoon about 1/2 cup sauce into each.
> Into each dish, carefully break two eggs over sauce. Top with 1 tablespoon melted butter.
> Bake in a preheated oven at 375 degrees 10-12 minutes or until eggs are cooked to desired hardness.
> Top each with 2 tablespoons cheese. Return to oven until melted. Serve hot.

Makes 12 servings

from **The Morical House**
668 North Main Street
Ashland, OR 97520
503-482-2254

    "Sometimes we serve this with a toasted English muffin under the cream sauce," said Innkeeper Pat Dahl, but either way, these eggs are something to celebrate. She devised the recipe for a special breakfast when honeymooners were among the guests. "I felt Eggs Benedict had been overdone, no pun intended," and poached eggs "can be tricky," so baked eggs worked perfectly.

    All of that goes to show that theater-goers are not the only ones who enjoy Ashland's B&Bs. Pat and Pete have served a number of travelers from "all over" who have enjoyed the five guestrooms in their 1880's home, the garden and the putting green, or nearby white water rafting and skiing.

Other Morical House recipes:
Pina Colada Smoothies, page 22
Walnut Frosties, page 139

Cheese and Bacon Frittata

Ingredients:

    6 eggs
    1 cup milk
    1 green onion, minced
    2 tablespoons butter or margarine, melted
    1/2 teaspoon salt
    1/2 teaspoon pepper
    4 ounces cheddar cheese, shredded
    1/2 pound bacon, cooked crisp and crumbled

> In a medium bowl, beat eggs, milk, onion, butter or margarine, salt and pepper with a wire whisk until well blended.
> Pour the mixture into a greased 9 x 9-inch baking pan.
> Sprinkle cheese and crumbled bacon evenly over the top.
> Bake in a preheated oven at 400 degrees for 20 minutes or until set and golden brown.

Makes 4 large servings

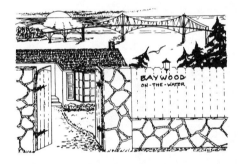

from **Baywood-on-the-Water**
4682 East Bay Drive
P.O. Box 1044
North Bend, OR 97459
503-756-6348

Servings of this hot breakfast casserole are welcomed by guests whether in the dining room or outside on the deck, overlooking Coos Bay and the mile-long McCullough Bridge. Herons, Canada geese, ducks, gulls, terns, osprey and an occasional bald eagle have been spotted during breakfast.

Scenery and outdoor recreation is a particular draw to North Bend. Innkeepers Caroline and Bob Kelley opened two guestrooms in 1984. Guests spend their days crabbing, clamming, surf fishing, deep sea fishing, inland fishing, whale watching, beachcombing and/or exploring tide pools. Those who want to learn something about the Oregon coast can visit the Oregon Institute of Marine Biology, the South Slough National Estuary Reserve, or the Oregon Dunes National Recreation Area.

Whatever their choice, guests look forward to returning here and having a long soak in the spa with a bay view.

Another Baywood-on-the-Water recipe:
Welsh Rarebit, page 129

Egg Souffle

Ingredients:

3/4 cup vegetables and/or cooked meat, diced very small (ham, bacon, green pepper, onion, shrimp, crab, smoked salmon and/or mushrooms work well)
Pepper
Nutmeg
3 eggs
2 tablespoons water
Salt
2 tablespoons colby cheese, grated

> In a bowl, combine meat, vegetables, pepper and nutmeg to taste.
> In a separate bowl, beat the eggs, water and salt with a wire whisk until fluffy.
> Pour the egg mixture into 2 custard cups three-quarters full.
> Place cups on a baking sheet. Bake in a preheated oven at 400 degrees for 10 minutes.
> Divide the vegetable/meat mixture evenly between the custard cups. Stir it into the semi-thickened eggs.
> Sprinkle the cheese on top. Return to the oven for 5 minutes or until the mixture puffs up above the top of the custard cup and cheese browns slightly.

Makes 2 servings

from **Chelsea Station**
4915 Linden Avenue N.
Seattle, WA 98103
206-547-6077

"The original recipe idea was found on a camping trip with friends to the deep woods of the Cascade Mountains just east of here," said Innkeeper Dick Jones. "Eggs were shipped with veggies and meat, then baked in the campfire coals inside tin cups. When they were opened, they were wonderfully puffed up!"

Since that time, Dick and Marylou have not been able to achieve quite the same puffiness (and nothing ever tastes as good as a hot campfire meal to hungry campers!). Dick has gone as far as trying carbonated water in the recipe, hoping the bubbles would make the little souffles puff up higher. While the bubbles didn't work, the souffle is still a tasty one-dish meal which guests enjoy at this urban B&B. Chelsea Station is a five-guestroom B&B in a 1920 brick home near Woodland Park Zoo.

Other Chelsea Station recipes:
Banana French Toast, page 106
Ginger Pancakes with Lemon Sauce, page 115

Eggs Artichoke

Ingredients:

6 English muffins, split and toasted
12 eggs, poached
12 slices Canadian bacon

Artichoke Sauce:
  2 tablespoons butter, melted
  3 tablespoons flour
  2-1/2 cups milk
  2 tablespoons vermouth
  1 cup plain artichoke hearts,
     drained and quartered
  Salt and pepper to taste

> First, make Artichoke Sauce: Cook the flour in the melted butter for 2-3 minutes.
> Gradually stir in the milk.
> Cook over medium heat, stirring constantly, until thickened.
> Add vermouth, unmarinated artichokes and salt and pepper. Blend well.
> Keep warm while poaching eggs, toasting English muffins and warming Canadian bacon.
> To assemble, place a Canadian bacon slice on each English muffin half, then top with a poached egg. Smother in Artichoke Sauce and serve.

Makes 6 large servings

from **Romeo Inn**
295 Idaho Street
Ashland, OR 97520
503-488-0884

"Most of our recipes are originals based on lots of research, testing and fine tuning," said Innkeeper Margaret Halverson. "This one, however, came as an overnight inspiration and has become a real favorite."

Margaret and Bruce share breakfast duties, working together to serve guests staying in their six guestrooms. Most guests are off to spend a day at the acclaimed Oregon Shakespearean Festival, only eight blocks away. But many come to enjoy the romantic rooms, with scented soaps, handmade quilts and country furnishings, or the swimming pool or hot tub.

Other Romeo Inn recipes:
Orange-Pineapple Braid, page 29
Food Processor Buttermilk Scones, page 39
Eggs Florentine, page 96

Eggs Benedict in Puff Pastry

Ingredients:
  Puff pastry shells or sheets
  4 eggs
  Butter
  Salt and pepper

Also:
  Hollandaise sauce (recipe on page 69)
  Paprika
  Bacon, crisp and crumbled
  Fresh lemon thyme or parsley

> Bake four individual puff pastry shells according to directions and remove centers. Or bake puff pastry sheets, cut in individual portions, and formed into a bowl-shape (place sheet of dough over a small, lightly greased oven-proof bowl, press down, bake in this "mold" according to package directions).
> Keep the pastry crispy in a 250-degree oven until ready for use.
> Poach four eggs with a small amount of butter. Extra large eggs need approximately 5 minutes to cook. Cook just until set; do not overcook. Salt and pepper to taste.
> Gently ease each poached egg into the center of the puff pastry shell or bowl.
> Top with Hollandaise sauce, sprinkle with paprika and bits of crisp bacon. Garnish with fresh lemon thyme or parsley.

Makes 4 servings

from **The Gallery B&B at
Little Cape Horn**
**4 Little Cape Horn
Cathlamet, WA 98612
206-425-7395**

Between the richness of homemade Hollandaise sauce and buttery puff pastry, one egg per person is plenty. Innkeeper Carolyn Feasey stretches breakfast out as a leisurely affair, encouraging guests to start with a beverage and muffin, take a stroll on the beach of the Columbia River outside the home, and then return for this dish, homemade Banana Mango Loaf and a fresh fruit compote. She finds guests really enjoy breakfast more that way.

Guests at this two-guestroom inn often are outside, enjoying the view or the stars from the deck, waving at tugboat captains, watching seals or windsurfers, or walking to a waterfall. Getting there can be half the fun, taking the ferry across the Columbia River or driving along the Long Beach.

Other Gallery B&B recipes:
Banana Mango Loaf, page 55
Homemade Hollandaise, page 69

Eggs Dungeness

Ingredients:

Fresh Dungeness crab
Old Bay seasoning
8 large English muffins, split
16 eggs, poached

Also:

Fresh chives
Parsley
Olives
Sweet peppers, chopped

Hollandaise Sauce:
4-6 egg yolks
2 tablespoons lemon juice
1/4 teaspoon white or cayenne
pepper
1/2 pound unsalted butter,
melted
1 tablespoon hot water
2-3 egg whites

> Boil crab with Old Bay seasoning. Cool and clean. This may be done the night before. Do not use canned crab.
> For Hollandaise Sauce: Combine yolks, lemon juice and pepper with a wire whisk in the top of a double boiler; then slowly whisk in butter. Add hot water to help stabilize the sauce. Remove from heat. In a separate bowl, beat egg whites until very stiff. With a wire whisk, fold egg whites into Hollandaise, only until incorporated.
> Toast split English muffins very lightly and poach eggs.
> Warm crab meat and place a healthy amount on English muffin halves, two per plate.
> Top crab with a poached egg. Lace with Hollandaise. Garnish with fresh chives, parsley, olives or chopped peppers.

Makes 8 servings

from **The Inn at Swifts Bay**
Port Stanley Road
Route 2, Box 3402
Lopez Island, WA 98261
206-468-3636

"We try to adjust our menus to what is available seasonally and locally. The crab comes from the San Juans, fresh from the Bay," said Innkeeper Chris Brandmeir. "The Eggs Dungeness are a great morning smell when the fresh ingredients are used." At this inn, they may be accompanied by hot lemon or cranberry muffins and organically-grown island raspberries.

Whipping up a delectable breakfast is no great chore for either Chris or co-innkeeper Robert Herrmann, both of whom have worked in many restaurants before entering innkeeping. Chris even has served as a brunch chef in Napa and San Francisco, and also cooked professionally in Seattle and on Lopez. They opened this four-guestroom inn in the spring of 1988.

Other Inn at Swifts Bay recipes:
Asparagus Herb Cheese Omelettes, page 88
Inn at Swifts Bay Potatoes, page 159

Eggs Florentine

Ingredients:

4 eggs, hard-cooked and sliced

Florentine Sauce:
- 2 tablespoons butter, melted
- 1 onion, chopped
- 2 tablespoons flour
- 2 cups milk
- 1 teaspoon hot pepper sauce
- Dash of salt
- Pinch of nutmeg
- 4 ounces fresh mushrooms, sliced
- 1 10-ounce package frozen chopped spinach, thawed and drained

Blender Hollandaise Sauce:
- 3 large egg yolks
- Dash hot pepper sauce
- Pinch salt
- 1-1/2 tablespoons lemon juice, fresh-squeezed
- 1/2 cup butter, melted

> For Hollandaise Sauce: Put all ingredients in blender except the butter. Blend at low speed.
> Pour in the butter in a slow, steady stream. Serve at room temperature (be sure to refrigerate leftovers).
> For Florentine Sauce: Melt the butter in a large skillet. Add onion and saute until soft.
> Stir in flour and cook over medium heat for 2-3 minutes.
> Gradually add the milk, stirring until the mixture boils and thickens.
> Stir in hot pepper sauce, salt and nutmeg, then mushrooms and spinach.
> To assemble: Evenly divide the spinach mixture between four ramekins which have been sprayed with a non-stick vegetable oil spray.
> Bake in a preheated oven at 350 degrees for 5-10 minutes, until bubbly.
> Arrange one egg over each dish of Florentine Sauce, then top with Hollandaise.

Makes 4 servings

from **Romeo Inn**
295 Idaho Street
Ashland, OR 97520
503-488-0884

Innkeeper Margaret Halverson called this dish "an elegant treat that also looks very attractive on the table." She and Bruce often serve it to guests staying in their six-guestroom inn, a 1930s Cape Cod home. "We grow our garnishes in our garden — variegated sage, basil, thyme, parsley. Eggs Florentine looks especially nice with edible nastursiums on the side."

Other Romeo Inn recipes:
Orange-Pineapple Braid, page 29
Food Processor Buttermilk Scones, page 39
Eggs Artichoke, page 93

Eggs Olympic

Ingredients:

    12 mushrooms, peeled or washed, then sliced
    4-1/2 tablespoons butter
    1 green onion, chopped
    8 eggs
    2 tablespoons water
    1/2 cup favorite tomato sauce
    1 cup cheddar cheese, shredded

> Saute sliced mushrooms in 1/2 tablespoon butter. Set aside.
> Melt 2 tablespoons butter in a large frying pan. Add onion and saute for 30 seconds.
> Beat eggs with the water. Pour into frying pan with onion, stirring continually.
> Just before the eggs "set," add remaining 2 tablespoons butter.
> Divide eggs into four ovenproof serving dishes.
> Top with mushrooms, tomato sauce and cheese.
> Just before serving, broil for 1 minute until the cheese melts and tomato sauce gets hot.

Makes 4 servings

from **Olympic Lights**
4531-A Cattle Point Road
Friday Harbor, WA 98250
206-378-3186

Innkeeper Lea Andrade has several hints for this recipe, including using a non-stick pan, which means using little or no butter. She also may use asparagus or ham in place of the mushrooms and change the cheese to jack or Swiss. And, she says, "I peel the mushrooms because I can be sure they are clean without getting them wet."

What home cooks may not be able to duplicate is the eggs, which she or husband Christian gather fresh from their Brahmas, Rhode Island Reds or Barred Rocks. Andrades seem to have been raising chickens and living on five acres in the San Juans forever, but it's only been since 1985, when they left the hustle and bustle of San Fransisco for life in the slower lane.

They and friends renovated this 1885 Victorian farmhouse, turning it into a five-guestroom B&B, which opened in 1986. Now, at about 8 a.m., instead of fighting traffic or co-workers, they are feeding appreciative chickens. Long ago, this farmhouse was home not only to chickens, but pigs, cattle and 11 children who enjoyed 320 acres of self-sustaining farm.

Another Olympic Lights recipe:
Cinnamon Swirls, page 58

Fancy Egg Scramble

Ingredients:

1 cup Canadian bacon, diced
1/4 cup green onion, chopped
3 tablespoons butter
12 eggs, beaten
1 3-ounce can mushroom pieces, drained
4 tablespoons butter, melted
2-1/2 cups soft bread crumbs
1/8 teaspoon paprika

Cheese Sauce:
2 tablespoons butter, melted
2 tablespoons flour
1/2 teaspoon salt
1/8 teaspoon pepper
2 cups milk
1 cup cheddar cheese, shredded

> First, make the Cheese Sauce: In a large saucepan, melt butter and blend in flour, salt and pepper. Whisk in milk, stirring until bubbly. Stir in cheese until melted. Set aside.
> In a large skillet, cook bacon and onion in 3 tablespoons butter until onion is tender, but not brown.
> Add eggs and scramble just until set.
> Fold eggs and mushrooms into Cheese Sauce.
> Turn mixture into a greased 7 x 12-inch baking dish.
> Combine 4 tablespoons melted butter, bread crumbs and paprika. Sprinkle over egg mixture.
> Cover and chill at least 30 minutes or overnight.
> Bake in a preheated oven at 350 degrees for 30 minutes, uncovered.

Makes 8 servings

from **Sonka's Sheep Station Inn**
901 NW Chadwick Lane
Myrtle Creek, OR 97457
503-863-5168

Garnished with assorted fruit, this makes a colorful morning entree, suggests Innkeeper Evelyn Sonka, who served this family favorite for years before opening four guestrooms on Sonka's sheep ranch in 1986.

Evelyn and Louis have a unique "farmstay" B&B in their 50-year-old farmhome with a wrap-around porch. They raise purebred and other sheep on 300 acres along the South Umpqua River in southwestern Oregon. Guests are invited to share in lambing, shearing, haying, helping with chores or just watching the border collies do their herding work. Instead of waking to an alarm or rooster, guests may be roused by lamb bleats and "baa's."

Another Sonka's Sheep Station Inn recipe:
Greek Ground Lamb Appetizers, page 157

Herb Garden Frittata

Ingredients:

1 medium onion, thinly sliced
1/4 cup olive oil
3 small zucchini, thinly sliced
6 eggs, beaten
1/2 teaspoon salt
1/2 teaspoon pepper
5 tablespoons parmesan cheese, grated
4 tablespoons butter
1 tablespoon fresh parsley, chopped
3-4 fresh basil leaves, cut into strips
1 tablespoon fresh oregano leaves, chopped

> In a skillet, saute onion in olive oil until transparent.
> Add zucchini and brown lightly.
> Reduce heat, let zucchini and onion cook down for 4-5 minutes. Drain oil off and cool.
> In a bowl, beat eggs with salt and pepper.
> Add zucchini and onion mixture and 4 tablespoons of the cheese.
> In a heavy ovenproof 10-inch skillet (black cast iron works best), heat butter until it foams.
> Pour egg mixture into the pan. Scatter the herbs on top.
> Keeping the heat very low, cook about 20 minutes until the eggs have barely set.
> Sprinkle with remaining cheese.
> Put pan under a hot broiler for 30-60 seconds.
> Run a sharp knife around the edge of the frittata to loosen it and slide it onto a warm plate.
> Cut in wedges to serve. "Equally good served warm, room temperature or chilled."

Makes 6 servings

from **Willowbrook Inn**
628 Foots Creek Road
Gold Hill, OR 97525
503-582-0075

At Willowbrook Inn, Innkeepers JoAnn and Tom Hoeber serve this frittata surrounded by purple and green basil and oregano leaves or chive blossoms. The herbs are among more than 100 varieties grown in an English-style herb garden on their 2.5 acres, complete with grass paths visitors can walk. Their inn is in a 1905 clapboard house built by a mining family.

Other Willowbrook Inn recipes:
Hot Vanilla, page 21
Gold Nugget Cakes with Peach Sauce, page 117

No-Crust Smoked Salmon Quiche

Ingredients:

4 eggs, beaten
1/2 cup butter, melted
1/2 cup buttermilk baking mix
1-1/2 cups milk
1/2 cup sharp cheddar cheese, grated
1/2 cup Swiss cheese, grated
3/4 cup chopped or flaked smoked salmon

> Beat the eggs, butter, baking mix and milk together with a wire whisk.
> Butter a large pie pan or quiche pan. Pour in the egg mixture.
> Dot the mixture with the cheeses and salmon, pressing into the egg mixture if necessary to submerge the cheeses and salmon.
> Bake in a preheated oven at 350 degrees for 45 minutes. Cut in wedges to serve.

Makes 6-8 servings

from **Mildred's B&B**
1201 15th Avenue E.
Seattle, WA 98112
206-325-6072

"I usually tell guests that this is my $50 recipe," says Innkeeper Mildred Sarver, since she once had a variation of it printed in a magazine and earned $50. Guests who treasure Pacific Northwest smoked salmon — and she gets a lot of them at her Capitol Hill B&B — tell her it's worth at least that much!

Mildred's white Queen Anne Victorian home is right across the street from the 44-acre Volunteer Park, where guests can work off the quiche on the tennis courts. Most of her guests, however, choose to spend their visit at the Seattle Art Museum, a short walk, or downtown. Mildred usually advises them to walk the 20 minutes downtown — "it's all downhill" — and then catch the bus on the way back. The bus stop is at the front door, so even those unfamiliar with the city will know when they're "home."

Guests here really do have use of the home as if it were their own. Downstairs, they may have cookies in front of the fire or enjoy the large front porch.

Other Mildred's B&B recipes:
Bran Muffins with Sesame Seed, page 37
Grandma Jessie Bell's Scotch Shortbread, page 156

Pacific Northwest Breakfast Eggs

Ingredients:

7 eggs
3 tablespoons sour cream
2 tablespoons milk
3 tablespoons green pepper, chopped
2 tablespoons green onion, chopped
3 tablespoons smoked salmon or smoked cod
1/2 cup cheddar cheese, grated
Salt and pepper

> Butter four ramekins or individual casserole dishes.
> Beat eggs with the sour cream and milk.
> Divide the eggs between the four baking dishes.
> Sprinkle with green pepper, green onion, smoked fish and cheddar cheese.
> Bake in a preheated oven at 350 degrees for 15 minutes.

Makes 4 servings

from **Home by the Sea**
2388 East Sunlight Beach Road
Clinton, WA 98236
206-221-2964

"This gets puffy and must be served immediately," said Innkeeper Sharon Fritts Drew. "I place this in the oven when my guests sit down to the fruit dish." The sour cream is a crucial addition, she said. And "because we live by the sea, guests come here with a desire for a taste of the sea."

Sharon and her mother, Helen Fritts, operate their home as a B&B and have several private guest cottages. Sharon returned to Whidbey Island after six years as a teacher at Tehran American School, leaving all her possessions behind in 1979. She had been able to return to Whidbey Island every summer while living in Iran, and finally bought property on the beach where she decided to put down more permanent roots.

Other Home by the Sea recipes:
Sharon's Beachside Banana Bread, page 63
Grandma Jenny's Norwegian Brown Cake, page 138
Pears Extraordinaire, page 147

Pesto Omelettes

Ingredients:

1 tablespoon butter or margarine
5 eggs
1/3 cup mozzarella cheese, shredded
2 tablespoons parmesan cheese, grated
4 tablespoons pesto (purchase commercially OR combine in a blender clean, fresh basil
    leaves, 1 or 2 cloves of garlic and olive oil to make a paste)

Also:

Tomato slices or wedges

> Melt butter in a hot omelette pan.
> With a fork, beat eggs. Continue beating as you pour eggs into the hot pan, and continue
beating until eggs start to solidify. Then spread eggs to cover the bottom of the pan.
> In a separate bowl, mix cheeses and pesto.
> Place pesto mixture on top of the omelette. Roll half of the set egg over on top to form the
omelette.
> Serve with tomato garnish.
> Note: To make one omelette, use 3 eggs, 1/4 cup mozzarella, 2 tablespoons parmesan
cheese and 2 tablespoons pesto.

Makes 2 servings

PORTLAND
GUEST HOUSE

from **Portland Guest House**
1720 NE 15th Avenue
Portland, OR 97212
503-282-1402

The basil for the pesto in this recipe comes from the herb garden around
Susan Gisvold's B&B. The garden complements the complete restoration of
this house, which Gisvold bought in 1986 to convert to a B&B. Working with
an architect and restoration contractor, she completed major work on the
1890 Victorian home, which was built when the street car line ended at 15th
and Broadway. During the construction process, discoveries behind old walls
included hats and hat pins, schoolbooks and children's notes and an 1895
Christian Endeavor hymnal.

Today, the home is one small gem in the neighborhood. It has four
guestrooms, and travelers are invited to enjoy the entire house, even to
invite a friend or associate in for a cup of tea. Gisvold, who has a degree in
home economics, will recommend shops and restaurants along Broadway in
the Irvington neighborhood. She also provides tickets for the city's model
light rail system for a 10-minute ride to downtown.

Another Portland Guest House recipe:
Oregon Hazelnut Sweet Rolls, page 62

Savory Baked Eggs

Ingredients:

1 cup fresh mushrooms, sliced, OR 1 4-ounce can sliced mushrooms, drained
12 eggs
2 cups cottage cheese
2 cups sharp cheddar cheese, grated
1 cup cooked ham, diced (or cooked bacon or sausage)
1/2 cup green onions, chopped
1 4-ounce can black olives, drained and sliced
1/2 cup green pepper, chopped, optional

> If fresh mushrooms are used, saute them first.
> Beat eggs with a wire whisk until light and fluffy.
> Whisk in cottage cheese.
> Whisk in other ingredients.
> Pour into a greased 9 x 13-inch baking dish.
> Bake in a preheated oven at 350 degrees for 45 minutes or until a knife inserted in the center comes out clean.
> Note: This recipe easily can be cut in half, or made with only the first five ingredients. If half is made, bake in a 9-inch pie pan for 35 minutes, or in ramekins for 20 minutes.

Makes 10 servings

from **Stange Manor B&B**
1612 Walnut Street
LaGrande, OR 97850
503-963-2400

The egg dish, easily modified to suit personal preferences, often is served in the dining room of this grand old home, which once took up a complete city block with tennis courts, ponds and stables of lumber baron August Stange.

Lynn and Steve Hart bought the huge Georgian Colonial "because it had been empty for a few years and was starting to deteriorate. We loved the home and wanted to preserve it, but it is so large we knew we couldn't afford to heat and maintain it," Lynn said. The five-guestroom mansion, which required a lot of tender loving restoration before opening in 1986, measures 12,000-square-feet. "We also own a restaurant and knew that we liked working with people."

LaGrande was an Eastern Oregon "oasis in the wilderness" for pioneers along the Oregon Trail. Today it offers visitors fishing, flightseeing, river rafting, skiing, pack trips and hot springs resorts.

Another Stange Manor recipe:
60 Minute Cinnamon Rolls, page 64

Souffle Roll

<u>*Ingredients:*</u>

4 tablespoons butter
1/2 cup flour
1 teaspoon salt
Pepper to taste
2 cups milk
5 eggs, separated

<u>*Also:*</u>

Waxed paper

Filling:

1 bunch cleaned fresh
spinach, chopped OR 1
10-ounce package frozen
chopped spinach
1 pound mushrooms, sliced
2 tablespoons butter
8 ounces cream cheese
Salt and pepper to taste

> Melt butter in a saucepan. Blend in flour, salt and pepper.
> Whisk in the milk, bringing the mixture to a boil. Stir constantly until thickened.
> Cool. Add the egg yolks and beat.
> In a separate bowl, beat the egg whites until stiff. Fold them into the cooled sauce.
> Line a greased jelly roll pan with waxed paper, then butter and flour the waxed paper.
> Pour the souffle mixture over the waxed paper, spreading lightly to form an even layer.
> Bake in a preheated oven at 400 degrees for 30 minutes or until nicely browned.
> While souffle is baking, make the Filling: Saute the spinach and mushrooms in butter until tender. Add the cream cheese and mix well. Season to taste. Set aside but keep warm.
> Turn souffle immediately onto a towel. Carefully remove waxed paper. Roll up lengthwise with the towel inside.
> After a minute or so, unroll. Spread filling evenly over the souffle. Roll up jelly roll-style with the help of a towel, this time *without* the towel inside. Serve immediately.
> This can be made the night before and reheated at 325 degrees in the morning.

Makes 6 servings

from **Turtleback Farm Inn**
Crow Valley Road
Route 1, Box 650
Orcas Island, WA 98245
206-376-4914

"This is my mother's recipe and is one of the most elegant breakfasts we serve," said Innkeeper Susan Fletcher. Susan and Bill moved to Turtleback, which is set on 80 rolling acres, and opened seven restored guestrooms in 1985. Now the farmhouse has special touches, like crystal doorknobs and no-peek keyholes from the old Seattle Savoy Hotel and pedestal sinks from the Empress Hotel in Victoria.

Other Turtleback Farm Inn recipes:
Sesame Corn Muffins, page 48
Cornmeal Waffles, page 121
Applesauce Bread Pudding, page 143

South of the Border Quiche

Ingredients:
8 eggs
1/4 cup flour
1 teaspoon baking powder
1/2 pound monterey jack cheese, grated (2 cups)
1/2 cup cottage cheese
1/4 cup butter or margarine, melted
1 4-ounce can green chili peppers, diced

Also:
Sour cream
Salsa

> Beat the eggs. Add flour and baking powder.
> Fold in cheeses. Mix well.
> Stir in melted butter and chilis.
> Pour the mixture into a greased quiche pan.
> Bake in a preheated oven at 350 degrees for 35 minutes.
> Cool for about 10 minutes. Serve wedges with a dollop of sour cream and salsa.

Makes 6-8 servings

from **Salisbury House**
750 16th Avenue E.
Seattle, WA 98112
206-328-8682

Innkeepers Mary and Cathryn Wiese lived for 18 years in southern California, where Cathryn was born, and they developed a love of Mexican and southwestern food. This recipe was given to them by a San Diego friend. At the B&B, it's served with a tropical fruit compote and corn muffins.

Guests enjoy breakfast in the dining room of this large Capitol Hill house. Downstairs, the home has refinished maple floors and wood beam ceilings. Upstairs are four guestrooms, all decorated in different color schemes, and a sun porch. Guests are welcome to play chess in the library, "set a spell" on the wrap-around porch, or enjoy the fireplace in the living room.

Other Salisbury House recipes:
Ginger Pear Muffins, page 40
Whole Wheat Irish Soda Bread, page 66
Mary's Citrus French Toast, page 108

Banana French Toast

Ingredients:
    2 eggs
    1/4 cup milk
    1 ripe banana
    1/2 teaspoon cinnamon
    1/2 teaspoon nutmeg
    6 thick slices French bread

Also:
    Bananas, sliced
    Coconut, toasted

> In the blender, combine all ingredients except the bread. Blend until smooth.
> Pour the batter into a pie plate. Soak one side of the bread, then flip to coat the other.
> Fry on a greased griddle at 250 degrees. When one side is golden brown, flip and fry the other.
> Serve with sliced bananas and toasted coconut (to toast coconut, spread in a pan and bake at 350 degrees for 10 minutes or until it turns light brown).

Makes 2-3 servings

from **Chelsea Station**
4915 Linden Avenue N.
Seattle, WA 98103
206-547-6077

Marylou and Dick Jones have been serving this recipe to guests since they opened their B&B in 1984, though they usually multiply it by five to feed a houseful. For an unusual syrup that they say goes well with the banana and spices, they melt six ounces of butterscotch candies into 18 ounces of imitation maple syrup.

When they bought their 1920 brick home, it had been converted to apartments. So they converted it back, with five guestrooms becoming suites that once were entire apartments. Marylou and Dick, a former hospital administrator, opened the inn to change their own lifestyle, which had been too stressful. Now they live a short walk from the Woodland Park Zoo and directly across from the Rose Gardens, and Dick has learned a bit about roses by tending more than two dozen species himself. The B&B also is within walking distance of Green Lake, several fine restaurants, the Chittenden Locks in Ballard and the Shilshole Bay Marina.

Other Chelsea Station recipes:
Egg Souffle, page 92
Ginger Pancakes with Lemon Sauce, page 115

Fluffy Fingers French Toast

Ingredients:
1 cup flour
1 teaspoon baking powder
1/2 teaspoon salt
1 cup milk
2 eggs, well beaten
10 slices white bread, crusts trimmed

Orange Syrup:
1 cup orange juice
1 cup sugar

Also:
Vegetable oil or shortening for frying
Powdered sugar

> First, make the Orange Syrup: In a small saucepan, mix orange juice and sugar. Bring to a boil and boil for five minutes. Set aside.
> In a separate bowl, sift flour with baking powder and salt.
> Stir in milk and eggs. Beat well.
> Cut each bread slice in thirds ("fingers") lengthwise.
> In a large frying pan, heat 1/2-inch of vegetable oil.
> Dip bread fingers into batter. Fry until light brown on both sides.
> Drain fingers and keep warm while frying all.
> Arrange on a heated platter and sprinkle with powdered sugar.
> Serve with Orange Syrup.

Makes 6 servings

from **Ahlf House B&B**
762 NW 6th Street
Grants Pass, OR 97526
503-474-1374

"This is light and delicious," said Innkeeper Betty Buskirk, who has served this favorite recipe many times for her own family and transferred it successfully to her B&B.

She and partner Rosemary Althaus opened their three-guestroom B&B in 1986. It is in the stately home of Susanah and Johan Ahlf, started in 1898 and completed in 1902 as a wedding present from Johan to his bride. Johan was one of the town's first butchers. The home, listed on the National Register of Historic Places, remains the largest Queen Anne Victorian house in town. It has been painted slate blue, with white, light blue and dark brown outlines of the considerable gingerbread.

Another Ahlf House recipe:
Quick Cobbler, page 161

Mary's Citrus French Toast

Ingredients:

1 loaf day-old French bread
6 to 8 eggs, well-beaten
2 tablespoons sugar
Grated rind of 2 large oranges
1/2 teaspoon vanilla extract
1-1/2 cups half-and-half

Also:

Powdered sugar
Orange slices
Maple syrup, warmed, with a shot of Triple Sec, optional

> The night before serving, slice the bread into 1-inch slices.
> The next morning, mix all ingredients except bread in a large, shallow bowl.
> Soak bread slices thoroughly in the mixture.
> Heat a greased griddle to 350 degrees.
> Fry each slice of bread 3-5 minutes on each side, until egg is cooked and golden brown.
> Place toast on warm plates, sprinkle with powdered sugar and garnish with a slice of orange. Serve with maple syrup.

Makes 6-8 servings

from **Salisbury House**
750 16th Avenue E.
Seattle, WA 98112
206-328-8682

"Living in beautiful San Diego for more than 18 years, we entertained a lot of visitors, so opening a bed-and-breakfast inn was a natural for us," said Innkeeper Cathryn Wiese. "This French Toast recipe was a popular one in California, where we had our own citrus trees, and remains a popular one here at Salisbury House."

Mary, who was raised in Seattle, and Cathryn, who has been in Seattle for the past decade, opened their B&B in 1984. They encourage guests to leave the car parked and walk to the Seattle Art Museum, Volunteer Park, shops and restaurants, or take the bus a block away to get downtown or to the University of Washington. Salisbury House is in a neighborhood of beautiful homes and large trees, including a tulip tree said to be the largest in the city.

Other Salisbury House recipes:
Ginger Pear Muffins, page 40
Whole Wheat Irish Soda Bread, page 66
South of the Border Quiche, page 105

Northwest Logs (French toast)

Ingredients:

1 8-ounce carton frozen egg substitute, thawed
   (or 3-4 eggs, beaten)
1 cup skim milk
2 tablespoons sugar
1 teaspoon orange-flavored liqueur
Day-old baguette of French bread, crusts
   trimmed and cut into 2 x 5-inch "logs"

Blueberry Compote:
   1 quart (4 cups) blueberries
   1/4 cup sugar
   2 tablespoons corn syrup
   1-2 teaspoons lemon juice
   1 teaspoon lemon peel, grated

Also:

Margarine or butter, melted
Toasted hazelnuts, coarsely chopped

> First, make the Blueberry Compote: Crush half the berries in a saucepan. Add remaining berries, sugar, corn syrup, lemon juice and peel. Cook, stirring often, over medium or low heat until slightly thickened.
> In a medium bowl, thoroughly mix egg substitute, milk, sugar and liqueur.
> Place bread "logs" on a jelly roll pan or baking pan with sides. Pour mixture over bread.
> In a few minutes, turn logs so all sides have soaked up liquid.
> At this point, "logs" can be frozen. Freeze "logs," uncovered, until solid enough to be placed in freezer bags.
> To cook, place as "logs" on a lightly-greased baking sheet.
> Brush with melted butter.
> Bake in a preheated oven at 450 degrees for 15-20 minutes.
> Turn "logs," brush with additional butter. Continue to bake another 5 minutes or so until nicely browned. Serve topped with Blueberry Compote and toasted hazelnuts.

Makes 4 servings

from **Orchard View Inn**
16540 NW Orchard View Road
McMinnville, OR 97128
503-472-0165

This recipe of the original innkeeper, Carole Barton, emphasizes wholesome, locally-grown foods low in cholesterol. Marie Schatter, who purchased Barton's inn with her husband, Wayne, has added her Blueberry Compote to the recipe and serves it to their B&B guests.

The octagon-shaped home, located five miles from McMinnville, has four guestrooms. All have views of the countryside and woods, and Mt. Hood is visible from the dining room window. Schatters chose innkeeping as a second career after retiring recently.

Strawberry French Toast

Ingredients:
3 eggs
3 tablespoons strawberry preserves
3/4 cup half-and-half
8 slices French bread, sliced 1/2-inch thick
1 quart (4 cups) fresh strawberries, cleaned and sliced

Strawberry Butter:
1/3 cup strawberry preserves
4 tablespoons butter, softened

Also:
Powdered sugar
Almonds, toasted and slivered

> Combine and beat the eggs, preserves and half-and-half.
> Layer bread one-slice-deep in a 9 x 13-inch glass baking dish.
> Pour egg mixture over the bread until all of it is covered.
> Cover dish and refrigerate overnight.
> To make the strawberry butter, blend ingredients in a food processor until fluffy.
> Fry bread on a buttered medium-hot griddle. After turning to cook the other side, generously cover the browned side with strawberry butter.
> To serve, place two slices of French toast on each plate, top with strawberries and almonds and dust with powdered sugar.

Makes 4 servings

from **Hersey House**
451 North Main Street
Ashland, OR 97520
503-482-4563

Fresh Oregon strawberries are featured in this breakfast entree at the Hersey House. Innkeepers and sisters Gail Orell and Lynn Savage try to feature Oregon specialties throughout their B&B, especially those made in Ashland. Guests will find the cheese and butter are from a local creamery and the flour in their recipes is from an Oregon mill that still stone-grinds wheat. Art work in the four guestrooms is by Oregon artists and the hand-wrapped glycerin cream soap is made in Ashland, too.

Served with steaming fresh-ground coffee, breakfast is enjoyed family-style at the dining room table in this 1904 home. Guests dine on family china amid antiques, leaded glass and natural woodwork.

Other Hersey House recipes:
Homemade Hot Mulled Cider, page 20
Gingerbread Pancakes, page 116
Plum Cheese Blintzes, page 127
Cranberry Sherbet, page 136

Surprise French Toast

Ingredients:

1 loaf French bread, at least one day old
4 eggs, lightly beaten
2 tablespoons milk
2 tablespoons Triple Sec
1 tablespoon maple syrup
1/2 teaspoon nutmeg
1-1/2 teaspoons orange peel, grated

Also:

Favorite preserves or Festive Marmalade (recipe on page 70)
Safflower oil
Powdered sugar
Maple syrup, optional

> Slice bread into 8 slices, each 1-1/2 inches thick. Slit a "pocket" into each slice, being careful not to cut all the way through.
> Spread 1 tablespoon preserves or marmalade inside pocket.
> In a pan, combine eggs with milk, Triple Sec, maple syrup, nutmeg and orange peel.
> Dip each slice of bread in the egg mixture.
> Fry in very shallow safflower oil on each side until golden brown.
> Dust with powdered sugar. Serve with warm maple syrup on the side.

Makes 8 servings

from **Cedarym**
1011 240th Avenue NE
Redmond, WA 98053
206-868-4159

"Surprise French Toast was created after our daughter came home from a motor trip and raved about a 'filled French toast' she had ordered in a restaurant. It had been filled with cream cheese, she thought," recalled Innkeeper Mary Ellen Brown. "So we experimented with different fillings and egg combinations until we settled on our Surprise combination. It is rather sweet, but many of our guests still add maple syrup."

Guests enjoy this entree by the light of Mary Ellen's hand-dipped candles in the dining room in front of a fireplace. Mary Ellen and Walt have turned their retirement home into a two-guestroom B&B with a colonial theme, where the furnishings and decor are authentic to the 1700s.

Other Cedarym recipes:
Festive Marmalade, page 70
Christmas Stollen, page 134
Cedarym Oats, page 151

Apple Dutch Babies with Cinnamon Candy Syrup

Ingredients:

6 tablespoons margarine
2 apples, peeled and thinly sliced
6 eggs
1-1/2 cups milk
1 cup flour
2 tablespoons sugar
1 teaspoon vanilla extract
1/2 teaspoon salt
1/2 teaspoon cinnamon

Cinnamon Candy Syrup:
1/2 cup brown sugar, packed
1/4 cup sugar
1/4 cup water
1/3 cup red hot cinnamon
   candies
3/4 cup half-and-half

> Melt margarine in a 9 x 13-inch baking dish or four individual 9-inch au gratin dishes.
> Add apples to the dish and heat until margarine sizzles. Don't brown the apples.
> In the blender, whirl the rest of the pancake ingredients until mixed well.
> Pour batter over the hot apples. Bake in a preheated oven at 425 degrees until puffed and golden, about 25 minutes.
> Cut large pancake into squares or serve individual pancakes immediately with Cinnamon Candy Syrup (or powdered sugar and lemon wedges).
> For Cinnamon Candy Syrup: Bring sugars, water and candies to a boil, stirring often.
> Remove from heat and stir in half-and-half. Serve warm.

Makes 4-6 servings

from **The Willows B&B**
5025 Homesteader Road
Wilsonville, OR 97070
503-638-3722

Innkeeper Shirlee Key advises using individual au gratin dishes — hers are Pfaltzgraff stonewear — because the oven pancakes don't fall so quickly if she needs to keep them warm in the oven, with the heat turned off and door opened. "This way, they puff even higher and make a terrific presentation."

The eggs in this dish might come from some of Shirlee and Dave's Bantam chickens, and guests may find fresh raspberries from their garden also on the table. Keys "retired" into the B&B business in Wilsonville, after Dave took early retirement from Texaco Oil. In 1984, they built this home on two pretty acres they purchased in 1975, thinking they'd like the area. They liked it so well that they finished their lower level as a large guest suite, and opened in 1986 to allow others to share their enthusiasm for the area.

Another Willows B&B recipe:
Shortbread Cookies, page 162

Apple-Oatmeal Spice Pancakes

Ingredients:
1 egg, beaten
1/2 cup buttermilk
2 tablespoons salad oil
1/2 cup flour
1/2 cup quick-cooking oats
1 tablespoon sugar
1 teaspoon baking powder
1/2 teaspoon baking soda
1/2 teaspoon cinnamon
1/4 teaspoon nutmeg
1/2 cup apples (Golden Delicious or Granny Smith preferred), grated

Also:
Walnuts, whipped butter, syrup, sour cream and/or apple butter

> By hand, beat all ingredients except the apples, just until smooth.
> Fold in the grated apples.
> For each pancake, pour about 1/4 cup batter onto a hot, greased griddle. Turn pancakes as soon as they are puffed and full of bubbles, but before bubbles break. Cook until golden brown.
> Sprinkle with walnuts and serve with whipped butter, syrup, sour cream or apple butter.

Makes about 3 servings

from **Amy's Manor B&B**
Highway 153
P.O. Box 411
Pateros, WA 98846
206-923-2334

"I like to use this recipe because it uses the ingredient our Methow Valley is famous for: apples. My husband and I have a 25-acre apple orchard containing Golden and Red Delicious apples. The goldens I use in my recipe are right out of our orchard. I also surprise the guests with fresh, crisp apples in a basket next to their beds."

Innkeeper Barbara Nickell is the granddaughter of Amy Pinckney Neff, a Washington native who married and raised five children in this home. The stucco home is set on a sweeping lawn under large trees, overlooking the Methow River. On the 170 acres, chickens, goats, ducks, rabbits and horses are raised. Located 195 miles east of Seattle, the home was opened as a two-guestroom B&B by Barb and husband Rodney in 1986. Guests can gather eggs, cross-country ski, relax or play tennis without leaving the property.

Cottage Cheese Hotcakes

Ingredients:
>   3 eggs, separated
>   3/4 cup small curd cottage cheese
>   1/4 cup flour
>   1/4 teaspoon salt

Also:
>   Favorite jam
>   Sour cream

> In a large bowl, beat egg yolks until thick.
> Add cottage cheese and beat well.
> Stir in the flour and salt.
> In a separate bowl, beat egg whites until they are stiff. Fold into the batter.
> Pour batter onto a hot, greased griddle (if using electric griddle, heat to 380 degrees) for pancakes 3-4 inches wide.
> Cook on both sides until golden brown and the edges are dry to the touch.
> Serve immediately with 1 teaspoon sour cream and 1 teaspoon jam on each hotcake.

Makes 3 servings

from **Log Castle B&B**
3273 East Saratoga Road
Langley, WA 98260
206-321-5483

"I got this recipe from my husband's cousin Miriam over 30 years ago, and I never used it until we started our bed and breakfast," admits Norma Metcalf. "I can't believe I waited so long for something so yummy!"

Guests may wonder why they waited so long to try this B&B. Hand-built from logs on their land by Norma's husband, State Senator Jack, the three-story log home has two guestrooms in the octagonal "turret." Large windows offer panoramic views of Saratoga Passage, Mt. Baker and the Cascades.

Downstairs, guests can enjoy the large, open living area and sit by the stone fireplace. Guests are free to walk on the beach (it's a 1.5-mile stroll to Langley) or through the 60 acres of woods, which has some of the oldest-growth timber on Whidbey Island. Breakfast, which always includes Norma's homemade specialties, is served on a dining room table made from a slab of giant Douglas fir sporting the local brand.

Another Log Castle B&B recipe:
Maple Nut Bread, page 61

Ginger Pancakes with Lemon Sauce

Ingredients:

4 cups whole wheat and honey pancake mix (such as Krusteaz)

2 teaspoons ginger

1 teaspoon cinnamon

1/2 teaspoon nutmeg

1/4 teaspoon cloves

1 tablespoon molasses

3-1/3 cups water

Lemon Sauce:

1 cup sugar

2-1/2 tablespoons cornstarch

2 cups water

4 tablespoons butter

4 tablespoons lemon juice

2 tablespoons lemon peel, grated

> For Pancakes: In a large bowl, combine all pancake ingredients. Blend until smooth and thick using a wire whisk.

> Pour batter onto a hot, greased griddle. Turn when bubbles show through and the edges are crispy. Cook on other side until golden brown.

> For Lemon Sauce: In a medium saucepan, combine sugar and cornstarch. Mix well.

> Stir in water gradually. Bring to a boil and cook over medium heat, stirring constantly, for about 5 minutes or until thick.

> Remove from heat. Stir in butter, lemon juice and lemon peel. Serve warm over pancakes. (The warm sauce is also good poured over gingerbread for dessert or snacks.)

Makes 6 servings

from **Chelsea Station**
4915 Linden Avenue N.
Seattle, WA 98103
206-547-6077

This pancake recipe is simple for rushed mornings, and the lemon sauce makes it special, said Innkeepers Marylou and Dick Jones. It is served to guests along with fresh fruit and fresh-ground coffee. Guests needn't worry about going hungry here at any time.   A "bottomless cookie jar" is open to guests 24 hours a day, as are coffee, tea and hot chocolate.

Food is never far from the inn, either. Good restaurants featuring Pacific Northwest seafood and other specialties are within walking distance, and the inn is only five minutes from downtown Seattle's restaurants and Pike Place Market, or the International District's outstanding Asian restaurants. Guests who don't care to drive can hop a bus at a nearby stop.

Dick and Marylou like to make the stay at the inn especially pleasant. A hot tub is located in the carriage house for private use by guests. Snacks or beverages can be stored in the refrigerator.

Other Chelsea Station recipes:
Egg Souffle, page 92
Banana French Toast, page 106

Gingerbread Pancakes

Ingredients:

2-1/2 cups flour
5 teaspoons baking powder
1 teaspoon baking soda
1-1/2 teaspoons salt
1 teaspoon cinnamon
1/2 teaspoon ginger
2 eggs
2 cups milk
1/4 cup molasses
1 cup raisins

Lemon Curd:
3 eggs
1/2 cup sugar
2/3 cup fresh lemon juice
6 tablespoons butter, melted
Zest (peel) of 2 lemons, grated

Also:

Plenty of butter for grilling

> In a large bowl, combine the flour, baking powder, soda, salt, cinnamon and ginger.
> In a separate bowl, beat eggs slightly. Then stir in milk and molasses.
> Pour egg mixture into dry ingredients. Stir only until moistened.
> Stir in raisins.
> Pour pancakes onto a well-buttered griddle. Flip when bubbles show through (these pancakes are dark so don't use color as a guide for when to flip).
> For Lemon Curd: Combine eggs, sugar and lemon juice. Add melted butter and mix well. Microwave on low, stirring every 2 minutes, until thick. Stir in zest.
> Serve warm on top of pancakes.

Makes 5 servings

from **Hersey House**
451 North Main Street
Ashland, OR 97520
503-482-4563

Innkeeper and Chief Cook Gail Orell has been collecting favorite recipes since she was a child and she continued all through her years as a flight attendant, before she and sister Lynn Savage opened Hersey House in their hometown. While Gail's tastes include exotic international cuisine, these aromatic, flavorful pancakes are an example of simple, down-home cooking she also enjoys. They are especially appreciated on chilly mornings by guests at this four-guestroom inn.

Other Hersey House recipes:
Homemade Hot Mulled Cider, page 20
Strawberry French Toast, page 110
Plum Cheese Blintzes, page 127
Cranberry Sherbet, page 136

Gold Nugget Cakes with Peach Sauce

Ingredients:

5 tablespoons margarine
1 cup nonfat milk
2 eggs, beaten
1-1/4 cups flour
4 teaspoons baking powder
3/4 teaspoon salt
1 tablespoon powdered ginger
6 ounces crystallized ginger, cut in 1/4 inch pieces

Peach Sauce:
1 tablespoon cornstarch
1/4 cup sugar
2 cups fresh or frozen
   peaches, sliced
2 tablespoons lemon juice
1/3 cup water (or use part
   peach-flavored liqueur)

> For Peach Sauce: Mix cornstarch and sugar in a saucepan. Add other ingredients and cook, stirring constantly, until the mixture has thickened. Keep warm.
> For Gold Nugget Cakes: Add margarine to milk. Heat until margarine melts, then cool slightly.
> Stir cooled milk mixture into beaten eggs. Mix well.
> In a separate bowl or on waxed paper, mix flour, baking powder, salt and powdered ginger.
> Add dry ingredients to egg mixture. Stir until blended.
> Pour about three tablespoons of batter per pancake onto a hot greased griddle.
> Sprinkle 1 teaspoon diced crystallized ginger on each pancake.
> When bubbles appear, flip pancake and cook for another 30 seconds on other side.
> Serve hot with warm Peach Sauce or real maple syrup.

Makes 6 servings

from **Willowbrook Inn**
628 Foots Creek Road
Gold Hill, OR 97525
503-582-0075

"Eureka! Being in the historic gold mining area of Gold Hill, it seemed natural that Willowbrook Inn should serve these pancakes highlighted with discoveries of bits of golden crystallized ginger in them," said Innkeeper JoAnn Hoeber. Gold was discovered in nearby Jacksonville in 1851, starting a 50-year boom. "Even today there is an active gold dredge in the Rogue River," said Tom Hoeber. "We have gold pans here at the inn and guests are encouraged to try their hand at panning in Foots Creek at the back of our property." Hoebers discovered their home while looking for property close to Ashland's Oregon Shakespeare Festival but rural enough to have gardens and animals. It took two years to turn the home into their B&B.

Other Willowbrook Inn recipes:
Hot Vanilla, page 21
Herb Garden Frittata, page 99

Mother's Buttermilk Pancakes

Ingredients:
> 2 eggs
> 1/4 cup vegetable oil
> 2-3/4 cups buttermilk
> 2 cups flour
> 1-1/4 teaspoons baking soda
> 3/4 teaspoon baking powder
> 1/4 teaspoon salt

Also:
> Jams, berry syrups, maple syrup or honey

> Beat eggs with a wire whisk.
> Beat the oil and buttermilk into the eggs until well-blended.
> Sift together flour, soda, baking powder, salt.
> Stir dry ingredients into the egg mixture, stirring only enough to moisten.
> Pour pancakes onto a hot, greased griddle, turning when bubbles appear.
> Serve with jams, berry syrups, maple syrup or honey.

Makes 4 servings

from **McGillivray's Log Home
Bed & Breakfast**
**88680 Evers Road
Elmira, OR 97437
503-935-3564**

Innkeeper Evelyn McGillivray cooks up her mother's buttermilk pancakes for guests on her antique woodburning stove, making them from-scratch using this recipe for more than 50 years. Evelyn uses her mother's antique cast iron griddle, which she said came from Sears in the 1920s and cost 29 cents.

Guests find that the rest of their stay in the old-fashioned log home has all the modern comforts. Guestrooms have king-size beds, private baths and air conditioning, and the upstairs room has its own outside deck and a skylight.

The log house was built by Evelyn and her late husband, and it is situated on five wooded acres 14 miles west of Eugene, on the way to the Oregon coast. Pheasants, jackrabbits and an occasional deer are seen amid the firs and pines. McGillivrays opened the home as a B&B in 1984, two years after construction was finished.

Norwegian Pancakes with Lingonberry Cream

Ingredients:

1-1/2 cups milk
2 eggs
1 cup flour
1/2 teaspoon salt
3 tablespoons butter, melted

Also:

Butter for frying

Lingonberry Cream:
1/2 cup lingonberry jam
1 cup heavy cream, whipped

> In the blender, mix milk and eggs. Then add flour and salt. Then blend in butter.
> Let batter rest for 30 minutes. Meanwhile, prepare Lingonberry Cream: To about 1 cup stiffly whipped cream, fold in about 1/2 cup lingonberry jam. Refrigerate until serving.
> To cook pancakes, heat a frying pan until a drop of water sizzles. Melt 1/2 teaspoon butter in the pan.
> Pour batter on the griddle in thin layers for each pancake.
> When dry on top, turn over and cook for 1 minute.
> Remove with a spatula to a warm platter. Roll the pancake up like a fat cigar.
> Continue until all batter is gone. Keep pancakes hot in oven set on the lowest heat.
> Arrange on a platter and sprinkle with powdered sugar. Serve with generous dollops of Lingonberry Cream.

Makes 3-4 servings

from **Marit's B&B**
6208 Palatine Avenue N.
Seattle, WA 98103
206-782-7900

When Innkeeper Marit Nelson serves this, her table is set in the red, white and blue colors of Norway, her Norwegian doll is in proper costume and acting as centerpiece, along with the Norwegian flag, and "my guests learn a lot about Norway!" Marit was born there and her taste for "tyttebaer krem" (Lingonberry Cream) has inspired many an American palate. (No other fruit jam combined with whipped cream has the same delicious taste.)

Actually, her table is changed every day, as Marit is a collector of fine china, and the Norwegian "Hearts and Pines" pattern comes out at Christmas. She and husband Carl, who opened their two-guestroom B&B in 1982, enjoy sharing their home with guests from all over. Their home in the Woodland Park neighborhood overlooks Puget Sound and the Olympic Mountains.

Other Marit's B&B recipes:
Golden Raisin Scones, page 41
Good and Good-for-You Yummie Cookies, page 155

Ricotta Cheese Pancakes

Ingredients:

3 eggs, separated
1/4 cup flour
3/4 cup ricotta cheese
2 tablespoons sugar
1/4 teaspoon salt
1 tablespoon lemon zest (peel), grated
1/4 cup butter or margarine, melted

Also:

Favorite berry sauce or berry syrup

> In a large bowl, mix egg yolks and the rest of the ingredients thoroughly.
> In a separate bowl, beat the egg whites until stiff.
> Fold egg whites into pancake batter.
> Pour batter onto a hot, greased griddle (325 degrees), turning when bubbles appear. Cook
on the other side until lightly browned.
> Serve hot with berry sauce or berry syrup.

Makes 3 servings

from **Eagles Nest Inn**
3236 East Saratoga Road
Langley, WA 98260
206-321-5331

The breakfast prepared by Innkeepers Nancy and Dale Bowman, often served
outside on decks with spectacular Puget Sound views, is just one thing to
"oooh" and "aaah" about here. Most guests began feeling a bit awestruck the
day before, after the ferry ride to Whidbey Island. They drove up to the top
of the hill and saw the three-story octagonal home, tucked away on 2.5 acres
of pines, that was four years in the planning. Inside, especially impressive
is the living room with a 17-foot cathedral ceiling. Also, the Eagles Nest
guestroom has the entire top floor with a 360-degree view.

Bowmans were first introduced to Whidbey Island in the 1970s, and made
plans to retire there, but did not know then that they would be innkeepers.
When they decided to build the B&B, they tried to make the most of the site
and the views of the water, which all three guestrooms, the kitchen and the
decks now enjoy. Dale did much of the building and installation himself.
Nancy was responsible for decorating, using pastels, wicker and antiques.

Other Eagles Nest Inn recipes:
Raspberry Muffins, page 46
Chip 'n Dale Chocolate Chip Cookies, page 153

Cornmeal Waffles

Ingredients:

2 eggs, separated
2 cups buttermilk
6 tablespoons butter, melted
1/2 cup unbleached flour
1/2 cup whole wheat flour
3/4 cup cornmeal
2 teaspoons baking powder
1 teaspoon baking soda
1/2 teaspoon salt
2 tablespoons sugar
1/4 cup wheat germ

Also:

Pure maple syrup, warmed

> In a blender, blend the egg yolks and buttermilk until smooth.
> Add the melted butter and blend again.
> In a large bowl, mix the dry ingredients. Then stir in the buttermilk mixture.
> Beat the egg whites until stiff but not dry. Fold them into the batter just until blended.
> Bake in a greased, preheated waffle iron. Serve hot with warm maple syrup and butter.

Makes 4-5 servings

from **Turtleback Farm Inn**
Crow Valley Road
Route 1, Box 650
Orcas Island, WA 98245
206-376-4914

These crispy waffles are a favorite at the farmhouse inn, where guests are fortified for a day of Orcas Island sea kayaking, wind surfing, golf, sailing, boating, biking or visiting weavers, painters and potters. Breakfast may be served in the large dining room or on a deck underneath an elm and near a stocked trout pond, from which guests (and ducks) may fish.

Guests discover this deep green farmhouse down an unpaved lane, six miles from the ferry landing. Susan and Bill Fletcher discovered it in 1984 while innocently looking for a summer home. Instead, they found a dilapidated house in need of much loving (and expensive) renovation and a full-time career as Orcas innkeepers. The restored house now has seven guestrooms.

Other Turtleback Farm Inn recipes:
Sesame Corn Muffins, page 48
Souffle Roll, page 104
Applesauce Bread Pudding, page 143

Melinda's Famous Wholegrain Waffles

Ingredients:

    9 eggs, separated
    4-1/2 cups water
    3/4 cup vegetable oil
    2 or 3 tablespoons honey ("None is OK, too.")
    6 teaspoons baking powder
    1 teaspoon salt
    4 cups whole wheat flour
    2 cups unbleached flour

Also:

    Naturally Sweet Fruit Syrup (recipe on page 72) or other syrups

> In a giant-sized bowl, beat the egg yolks with water.
> Add remaining ingredients (except egg whites) one at a time. Mix well after each addition.
> In a separate bowl, beat the egg whites until stiff. Fold into batter.
> Pour batter onto a hot greased waffle iron (400-degree). Bake 4-5 minutes or until the steaming stops. Lift waffle carefully with a fork.
> Serve with Naturally Sweet Fruit Syrup, pure maple syrup or other favorite toppings.

Makes 8-10 servings

from **Spring Creek Llama Ranch**
14700 NE Spring Creek Lane
Newberg, OR 97132
503-538-5717

"I make these waffles fresh on the weekends for B&B guests and freeze the uneaten waffles for the family for weekday mornings," said Innkeeper Melinda Van Bossuyt, who tries to use whole grains often in her cooking. "Sometimes I substitute 1 cup cornmeal for 1 cup of the whole wheat flour. Or I use all whole wheat pastry flour instead of whole wheat and white flours. All combinations are delicious." At the Ranch, waffles are topped with her homemade Naturally Sweet Fruit Syrups or real maple syrup.

Breakfast is served family-style here, and guests never leave the table hungry. "The record for the most waffles eaten is three-and-a-half, by a guest from Texas," Melinda noted. Fresh eggs from the hen house or homegrown produce may be included in the meal, and guests who wish can help gather the eggs.

Other Spring Creek Llama Ranch recipes:
Melinda's Whole Wheat Blueberry Muffins, page 43
Naturally Sweet Fruit Syrup, page 72
Our Favorite Oatmeal-Raisin Cookie, page 160

Norwegian Waffles

Ingredients:

3 eggs, separated
1-1/3 cups milk
1/2 cup buttermilk or plain yogurt
3 tablespoons margarine or butter, melted
1-2/3 cups flour
1-1/2 teaspoons baking powder
1/2 teaspoon cardamom
1 tablespoon sugar
A pinch of salt

Sauce:
1/2 cup plain yogurt
1/2 cup sour cream

Also:

Low sugar, fresh-frozen berry jams

> Mix egg yolks, milk and buttermilk or yogurt. Stir in butter.
> In a separate bowl, sift flour, baking powder, cardamom, sugar and salt. Then mix well into egg mixture.
> Beat egg whites until stiff. Fold gently into waffle batter.
> If using a heart-shaped Norwegian waffle iron (for sale in specialty stores or catalogs), spray lightly with non-stick spray. Heat the iron approximately three minutes on each side over medium high heat. (Batter can also be poured into an electric waffle iron.)
> Pour about 1/3 cup batter in the center of hot greased waffle iron and bake waffles until golden brown, about 3 minutes on each side.
> Serve warm (keep in a 200-degree oven) with the yogurt/sour cream mixture and jams.

Makes 5-6 servings

from **The Ward House B&B**
516 Redwood Street
P.O. Box 86
Brookings, OR 97415
503-469-5557

"Every Norwegian housewife often serves these heart-shaped waffles cold for drop-in guests, and everyone has their own batter mix according to availability of ingredients on the spur of the moment," explains Innkeeper Gro Lent. "When we opened our B&B four years ago, I decided to make it a specialty of the house. I developed the yogurt/sour cream sauce and my own berry jams. Blueberries, strawberries and raspberries come from our own garden. Blackberries and huckleberries are picked in the wild." Gro (pronounced "Grew") even serves these waffles to breakfast guests wearing her Norwegian costume, brought from her native Norway.

Other Ward House recipes:
Any Time Herbal Tea, page 18
Chocolate Sauerkraut Cake, page 145

Sourdough Waffles

Ingredients:

1 cup active sourdough starter, brought to room temperature
2 cups whole wheat flour (or substitute 2/3 cup oat bran for 2/3 cup flour)
2 cups water
2 teaspoons sugar
1 teaspoon salt
3 tablespoons sugar
2 egg yolks
2/3 cup nonfat dry milk
1/3 cup cooking oil
1/3 teaspoon baking soda
2 egg whites, beaten until soft peaks are formed

Also:

Berries, whipped cream, syrups, yogurt, coconut, other favorite toppings

> The night before serving, mix starter, flour, water and 2 teaspoons sugar with a wooden spoon. Set the bowl in a warm place and cover with a damp towel.
> In the morning, remove 1 cup of this new "starter." Store it in a covered pint jar in the refrigerator for the next batch.
> To the remaining new "starter" made the night before, stir in the rest of the ingredients, except the baking soda and egg whites, and stir with a wooden spoon.
> If the dough is very sour, add the baking soda.
> Fold in beaten egg whites.
> Pour batter into the hot greased waffle iron. Batter will be "on the thin side," but "it raises a lot in making nice crisp waffles."
> Serve on heated plates with a selection of toppings.

Makes 4-6 servings

from **Getty's Emerald Garden
Bed & Breakfast**
**640 Audel Avenue
Eugene, OR 97404
503-688-6344**

"We always serve these waffles until our guests say, 'No more!'" said Innkeeper Jackie Getty. Breakfast also includes bacon or sausage, fresh fruit and garden produce. Guests feast at the dining room table which belonged to Bob's grandparents. Gettys opened their two guestrooms in 1989 after traveling in B&Bs across Canada. Their contemporary home is in a country-like setting in the city, a half-block from swimming and hot tubbing at Emerald Park.

Blueberry Serenescene

Ingredients:

8 or more slices sourdough French bread
4 eggs, beaten
1/2 cup milk
1/4 teaspoon baking powder
1-1/2 teaspoons vanilla extract
1/2 cup sugar
1 teaspoon cinnamon
1/2 teaspoon allspice
1-1/2 teaspoons cornstarch
2 12-ounce packages frozen (dry pack) blueberries OR 4-1/2 cups fresh blueberries
2 tablespoons butter or margarine, melted

Also:

Powdered sugar

> Trim off bread crusts. Cut bread into 2 x 4-inch pieces. Arrange bread to fill tightly a 10 x 15-inch baking pan or rimmed sheet (re-cut bread pieces to fit as necessary).
> In a bowl, beat eggs, milk, baking powder and vanilla.
> Pour mixture over bread, turning to coat both sides. Cover with plastic wrap and refrigerate overnight.
> In the morning, in a large bowl, mix sugar, cinnamon, allspice and cornstarch. Fold in frozen (do not defrost) or fresh berries, coating all berries thoroughly.
> Place the berries in a greased 9 x 13-inch baking pan.
> Cover berries with as many pieces of the pre-soaked bread as needed. Drizzle with butter.
> Bake in a preheated oven at 450 degrees for 25 minutes, until bread is golden and berries are bubbly.
> Sift powdered sugar on top. Cover with foil and let sit for 5-10 minutes. When serving, scoop up berries from the bottom to cover the top, as well.

Makes 6-8 servings

from **Chambered Nautilus**
5005 22nd Avenue NE
Seattle, WA 98105
206-522-2536

Innkeeper Bunny Hagemeyer said this recipe reminds her of "the wonderful blueberry-covered hill in front of my mother's 'camp' in the Adirondacks. Four generations have enjoyed the communal collecting of blueberries for a multitude of wonderful breakfasts, lunches and desserts." Now they're on the menu at this six-guestroom inn, located in Seattle's University district.

Other Chambered Nautilus recipes:
Cinnamon Cream Syrup, page 68
Apple Quiche, page 87

Clafoute-style Bread Pudding

Ingredients:

8 ounces stale sourdough French bread,
    sliced 3/4-inch thick
1/2 cup raisins
2 eggs
1/3 cup sugar
3 cups milk (1% preferred)
2 teaspoons vanilla extract
1 teaspoon nutmeg, grated

Warm Berry Sauce:
    2 cups fresh berries
    1/4 cup sugar
    1/2 cup orange juice

> Arrange the bread slices one-layer deep and tightly fitted on the bottom of a 9 x 13-inch glass baking dish.
> Sprinkle the raisins on top.
> In a separate bowl, mix the eggs, sugar, milk and vanilla.
> Pour the mixture over the bread. Sprinkle with nutmeg.
> Cover and refrigerate overnight.
> In the morning, let the pan sit at room temperature for 15 minutes.
> Bake in a preheated oven at 350 degrees for 45 minutes, until lightly browned.
> Remove pudding from oven. Let it settle for 15 minutes.
> Slice into 8 rectangles and serve warm or at room temperature.
> For Warm Berry Sauce: In a sauce pan, mix berries (wild blackberries, strawberries and/or raspberries preferred), sugar and juice. Bring the mixture to a boil. Lower heat and cook for 20 minutes, stirring often. Serve in a bowl and ladle over the bread pudding.

Makes 8 large servings

MOON & SIXPENCE

from **Moon and Sixpence Inn**
3021 Beaverton Valley Road
Friday Harbor, WA 98250
206-378-4138

"My Clafoute is based on my grandmother's bread pudding recipe and the traditional French peasant dessert Clafoutis," said Innkeeper Evelyn Tuller. She significantly cut back on the butter and sugar from her Pennsylvania Dutch grandmother's recipe and serves it to guests as a breakfast entree.

It's common to find Pennsylvania Dutch treats on the menu here, where Ev and Charles have restored a farmhouse built in the early 1900s as their B&B. An acre of lawn surrounds the farmhouse, and this was once a dairy farm in the middle of San Juan Island. Tullers offer three guestrooms in the farmhouse, and two rooms and a weaving studio are in restored "outbuildings." The sheep from which the wool comes can be seen grazing in the pasture next to the house.

Plum Cheese Blintzes

Ingredients:

Crepes:
- 4 eggs
- 4 tablespoons butter, melted
- 2-2/3 cups milk
- 2 cups flour
- 1 teaspoon salt

Cheese Filling:
- 2 cups cottage cheese, strained
- 1 egg
- 2 tablespoons powdered sugar
- 1/2 teaspoon vanilla extract
- 1/4 teaspoon cinnamon
- 1 cup sour cream

Plum Sauce:
- 1/4 cup butter
- 1/2 cup sugar
- 2 teaspoons cornstarch
- 1/8 teaspoon nutmeg
- 4 cups fresh plums, quartered and pitted
- 1/2 teaspoon vanilla extract
- Juice and grated peel of 1 small orange

> For Crepes: In a blender, blend all crepe ingredients. Pour 1/4 cup batter per crepe into a non-stick pan. Turn after the top forms beads of moisture (just a few seconds). Cook briefly on the other side, then set crepes aside.

> For Plum Sauce: Melt butter in a large pot. Stir in sugar, cornstarch and nutmeg. Mix in plums, turning to coat with sugar. Stir occasionally over medium heat until juice forms a thick sauce (3-5 minutes). Remove from heat. Stir in vanilla, orange juice and peel. Return to heat and stir 2-3 minutes until sauce boils and thickens slightly. Strain sauce.

> For Cheese Filling: Blend all filling ingredients.

> To assemble blintzes: Put up to 2 tablespoons Cheese Filling in each crepe. Fold in the two sides, then the two ends, so the blintz is square.

> Place 3 tablespoons strained sauce on the bottom of an ovenproof plate. Add two blintzes and top with 1/3 cup of sauce. Bake in a preheated oven at 350 degrees for 20 minutes.

Makes 4 servings

from **Hersey House**
451 North Main Street
Ashland, OR 97520
503-482-4563

"This recipe was developed because we have three Thundercloud plum trees which bear fruit the size of a large cherry," said Innkeeper Gail Orell. "This would make an excellent holiday entree — very red."

Other Hersey House recipes:
Homemade Hot Mulled Cider, page 20
Strawberry French Toast, page 110
Gingerbread Pancakes, page 116
Cranberry Sherbet, page 136

Sea Bag Salmon

Ingredients:

1 whole salmon ("Cut off head and tail; gut and debone as best you can")
Onions, sliced
Lemon, sliced
Bacon, partially cooked
Up to 1/4 pound butter
Salt and pepper
Garlic powder or dried minced garlic
"Maybe beer and wine"

Also:

Paprika, dried seaweed, lemon wedges

> Rinse salmon. Inside of fish, line up sliced onions, slices of lemon and strips of bacon.
> "Use lots of pepper and a shake or two of garlic. Very little salt."
> Slice up to 1/4 pound butter, place on top of fish. Wrap fish in foil.
> "Plan B: You can use a fork and poke holes into the sides of the fish and put the bacon strips out there with the butter, next to the foil. Never hurts to add a little beer* [see below] or wine in there, too."
> Bake in a preheated oven at 350 degrees for 20 minutes.
> Garnish filets with paprika, dried seaweed and lemon wedges.

Makes 4-6 servings, depending on size of fish

KRESTINE
1904

from **Tall Ship Ketch Krestine**
3311 Harborview Drive
Gig Harbor, WA 98335
206-858-9395

*"Save a little of this back, and if nobody shows up, forget the damned fish and drink the beer straight!" advises Capt. Pete Darrah. This original fish recipe was "invented out of necessity 23 years ago when a friend dumped an extra salmon on me and I had to figure out what to do with it — it was my first salmon." Turned out good enough to eat.

Overnight guests come to enjoy the nautical atmosphere aboard the tall ship, built in 1904 and moored in Gig Harbor, "where specialty shops are a mere monkey fist heave from the ship's poop deck." Guests are awakened at a time agreed upon the night before, and Capt. Pete uses a "bos'n pipe, ship's bell and martial music" to do so. The mid-ship saloon is where the meal is served family-style, around a table seating eight, by the light of oil lamps.

Another Tall Ship Ketch Krestine recipe:
Captain Pedro's Private Stores, page 89

Welsh Rarebit

Ingredients:

3 tablespoons cornstarch
1/4 teaspoon dry mustard
1/4 teaspoon salt
1/4 teaspoon pepper
2 cups milk
3 tablespoons butter or margarine
1/2 tablespoon Worcestershire sauce
1/2 pound cheddar cheese, shredded

Also:

Scones, toast or cornbread

> In a two-quart saucepan, stir together cornstarch, mustard, salt and pepper.
> Gradually stir in 1/2 cup milk until smooth.
> Add remaining milk, butter and Worcestershire sauce.
> Bring mixture to boil over medium-low heat, stirring constantly. Boil 1 minute.
> Add cheese, about 1 cup at a time.
> Cook over low heat, stirring constantly, until all the cheese is melted.
> Serve over scones, toast or cornbread.

Makes 6-8 servings

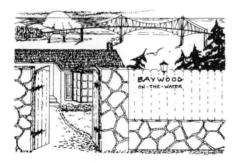

from **Baywood-on-the-Water**
4682 East Bay Drive
P.O. Box 1044
North Bend, OR 97459
503-756-6348

Innkeeper Caroline Kelley has adapted her mother's recipe for use in her B&B. She prefers to serve the sauce over cornbread and says her guests agree. "It is delicious served with fruit and a glass of orange juice. And it is easy — just be careful not to burn."

Caroline and Bob began innkeeping in 1984 in order to share their coast home with visitors from all over the world. They have stayed in many B&Bs in Europe and were the first to bring the concept back and open their own B&B in Coos County. Two guestrooms are available.

Kelleys direct guests to the many outdoor recreation areas, the myrtlewood factory or art galleries, museums and restaurants along Coos Bay.

Another Baywood-on-the-Water recipe:
Cheese and Bacon Frittata, page 91

Anyone who has had to travel over a major holiday can understand how it could be a depressing event. But holiday travel is done on purpose to many Pacific Northwest B&Bs. These wonderful homes are decorated to the rafters with boughs and bows for Christmas. Another holiday that's popular at romantic inns is Valentine's Day, where lovers treat themselves to rooms with whirlpools or a four-poster bed. Whatever the holiday, innkeepers rise to the occasion with fantastic fare. They've generously shared their treasured recipes so now those recipes can be a family tradition at home, as well.

Holiday Fare

Cherry Scones

<u>**Ingredients:**</u>
- 2 cups flour
- 2 tablespoons sugar
- 1 teaspoon baking powder
- 1/4 teaspoon salt
- 6 tablespoons butter, chilled
- 2 eggs
- 1/2 cup half-and-half or milk
- 1/2 cup maraschino cherries, drained and chopped

> In a large bowl, mix the flour, sugar, baking powder and salt.
> Chop the chilled butter. Then cut the pieces into the dry ingredients until it resembles coarse meal.
> In a small bowl, mix 1 egg with half-and-half or milk.
> Make a "well" in the center of the dry mixture. Pour in the egg mixture. Then add the cherries and stir until all the dough clings together.
> On a floured surface, knead the dough for 10-15 strokes.
> Roll out the dough to about 1/2-inch thick.
> Using a 2-inch heart-shaped cookie cutter, cut out scones. Place them close together on an ungreased cookie sheet.
> Beat the other egg slightly. Brush it on tops of the scones.
> Bake in a preheated oven at 400 degrees for 10-12 minutes, or until tops are light brown.

Makes 14-18 scones

from **The White Swan Guest House**
1388 Moore Road
Mount Vernon, WA 98273
206-445-6805

"These are pretty simple, but I think it's the heart-shaped cookie cutter I cut them with that makes people gobble them up," said Innkeeper Peter Goldfarb, who always serves these scones for Valentine's Day. He serves them with cream cheese for spreading, on a red-checked napkin in a basket, along with fresh-squeezed juice, fruit and hot coffee.

Peter restored this 1898 farmhouse and opened three guestrooms in the LaConner/Skagit River Valley in 1986. He moved here from New York, and is happy to share information on the area's many attractions with guests.

Christmas Hash

Ingredients:

    2 cups sausage, sliced (Polish, German, chorizo or mixture thereof)
    10 medium red potatoes, boiled and unpeeled
    4 large green onions, sliced with green tops
    1 sweet red pepper, diced
    1 green pepper, diced
    2 cups mushrooms, sliced thickly
    1/2 cup of mixture of fresh basil, cilantro and parsley, chopped
    1/4 cup parmesan cheese, grated
    Pinch of salt and pepper
    8 eggs, poached

> Fry sausage and drain.
> Fry other vegetables, herbs and spices.
> Mix sausage and other ingredients in a casserole dish. Sprinkle with cheese.
> Bake in a preheated oven at 375 degrees for about 10 minutes, just to blend the flavors and cheese.
> Serve with poached eggs on top.

Makes 8 servings

from **Riverbanks Inn**
8401 Riverbanks Road
Grants Pass, OR 97527
503-479-1118

This hash has just the right red and green colors to be a favorite Christmas dish of Innkeeper Myrtle Franklin, who opened this lodge on the banks of the Rogue River in 1988. Myrtle, who cooked for four years at the Esalen Institute in Big Sur, Calif., also can list social worker, counselor, art and music teacher, relief fund organizer, massage therapist and world traveler among her list of accomplishments, careers and interests before taking on innkeeping as a new adventure.

Myrtle bought the 14 acres on the river, located 15 miles from Grants Pass, with the idea of a spa, inn, artist retreat and fishing lodge. She completed substantial remodeling on the main house to add stone, wood and glass. In addition to enjoying breakfast, guests can row on the river-fed ponds, enjoy the wooden decks overlooking the river, soak in the whirlpool, work out in the exercise room, fish, or depart for raft trips. Accommodations are in the main house or in other cottages on the property.

Christmas Stollen

Ingredients:

- 4 cups flour
- 1 cup shortening
- 1 teaspoon salt
- 3 teaspoons sugar
- 3 eggs, separated
- 1 cup warm milk (no higher than 115 degrees)
- 1 package active dry yeast
- 16 to 24 ounces candied mixed fruit
- 1 cup walnuts or pecans, chopped
- 1 cup sugar
- 1/4 teaspoon cinnamon

Also:

- Butter, melted
- Powdered sugar

> Combine flour, shortening, salt and 2 teaspoons sugar and mix like a pie dough. Set aside.
> Dissolve yeast in warm milk with 1 teaspoon sugar.
> Beat the egg yolks. Stir into the milk and yeast.
> Add the liquid to the flour. Mix only until flour is moist. Cover and refrigerate overnight.
> In the morning, divide dough into six equal parts for small stollen or three parts for large.
> Beat egg whites until stiff, adding sugar and cinnamon gradually.
> Knead dough lightly and shape into balls.
> Roll out one dough ball on a floured board. Roll as thin as possible without tearing.
> Brush dough with a portion of egg whites. Sprinkle with a portion of nuts and fruit.
> Roll up like a jelly roll. Place on a greased baking sheet.
> Repeat with rest of dough. Let stollen rise in a draft-free area until they have doubled.
> Bake in a preheated oven at 325 degrees for 30 minutes for small stollen, longer for large.
> Brush with melted butter and dust with powdered sugar before serving.

Makes 24 servings, 6 small or 3 large stollen

from **Cedarym**
1011 240th Avenue NE
Redmond, WA 98053
206-868-4159

This family tradition of Innkeepers Mary Ellen and Walt Brown now is served to guests in the colonial dining room, lit by 12 hand-dipped candles. Browns have a fire in the brick fireplace, and the whole house is festively decorated.

Other Cedarym recipes:
Festive Marmalade, page 70
Surprise French Toast, page 111
Cedarym Oats, page 151

Cinnamon Pecans

Ingredients:

    1 pound (4 cups) pecan halves
    2 egg whites
    1 cup sugar
    2 tablespoons cinnamon

> Roll pecan halves in unbeaten egg whites until well-coated and slippery.
> In a separate pan, mix sugar and cinnamon.
> Drop pecans in sugar-cinnamon mixture. Roll until well-coated.
> Spread pecans on a greased cookie sheet.
> Bake in a preheated oven at 300 degrees for 15 minutes.
> Turn pecans over and bake on other side for another 15 minutes.
> Remove from oven, break apart and let dry.

Makes 4 cups

from **The Victorian B&B**
602 North Main Street
Coupeville, WA 98239
206-678-5305

This sweet treat has been one of Innkeeper Dolores Fresh's Christmas traditions for years, and now she shares it with holiday guests at the Victorian B&B on Whidbey Island.

In 1988, Dolores purchased this B&B, making a major change in her life. She was a special education teacher in the Los Angeles public schools, and she wanted to be closer to her son and family in Seattle. The B&B fit the bill.

Two guestrooms and a private cottage are available here. Bertha and Jacob Jenne, German immigrants, had this Italianate-style home built in 1889, using savings from years of farming. Two years later, they bought the Central Hotel on Front Street and became innkeepers.

The Coupeville home, in addition to being a fine structure, had several progressive features. It was said to be the first home on Whidbey Island to have running water, provided by the water tower still behind the house, and eventually the first to have oil-heated radiators circulating heat to each room, which still work today.

Another Victorian B&B recipe:
Cheese Olive Appetizers, page 152

Cranberry Sherbet

Ingredients:

4 cups fresh or frozen cranberries, washed
4 cups water
2-1/2 cups sugar
1 cup orange juice
1 teaspoon orange peel, grated
2 egg whites
1 tablespoon unflavored gelatin
1/4 cup cold water

> Place cranberries and water in a large cooking pot. Boil until tender, remove from heat.
> Press cooked cranberries through a sieve.
> Recook the sieved berries with the sugar, juice and peel for 5 minutes.
> Remove from heat and let thoroughly cool.
> In a large bowl, beat egg whites until stiff.
> In a separate bowl, stir the gelatin into the cold water. Let stand for 5 minutes only.
> Fold egg whites and gelatin into cold cranberry mixture.
> Pour mixture into shallow pans or ice cube trays without the cube compartments.
> Freeze, stirring once or twice when still "mushy" to mix well. Then freeze until firm.

Makes 12 servings

from **Hersey House**
451 North Main Street
Ashland, OR 97520
503-482-4563

"This is an old family recipe which always accompanied holiday turkey," said Innkeeper Gail Orell. "The sherbet was served as a side dish to accompany the meat. The third generation of our family now serves it to their families at holiday time." The sherbet also has special meaning because Gail and her sister, Lynn Savage, who run the inn together, grew up on the Oregon coast, one of the major cranberry-producing regions of the U.S.

Even if you're not related to this family (their grandfather was an early Ashland teacher), or to the Hersey family that raised five generations in the home, you'll feel that way after a stay in one of their four guestrooms. The sisters have completely redecorated and restored the 1904 home.

Other Hersey House recipes:
Homemade Hot Mulled Cider, page 20
Strawberry French Toast, page 110
Gingerbread Pancakes, page 116
Plum Cheese Blintzes, page 127

Eggnog French Toast Almondine

Ingredients:
4 eggs
1/4 cup sugar
3/4 cup half-and-half
1 tablespoon brandy
1/2 teaspoon vanilla extract
1/4 teaspoon nutmeg
8 slices French bread, 3/4-inch thick
6 tablespoons butter

Strawberry Sauce:
1 12-ounce package frozen
   strawberries, thawed
1 tablespoon sugar
1 tablespoon water

Also:
Slivered almonds

> For Strawberry Sauce: Mix ingredients in medium saucepan. Bring to a boil and simmer 5 minutes, crushing berries with a spoon. Remove from heat and cool slightly before serving.
> In a bowl, whisk together eggs and sugar.
> Whisk in half-and-half, brandy, vanilla and nutmeg.
> Place bread slices in a shallow baking dish.
> Pour egg mixture over the bread, turning slices to coat all sides.
> Cover and refrigerate overnight.
> In the morning, remove slices and coat both sides with almonds.
> Melt butter and cook French toast on a griddle over medium heat until golden brown on both sides.
> Serve with warm Strawberry Sauce.

Makes 4 servings

from **The Pringle House B&B**
Locust at 7th Streets
P.O. Box 578
Oakland, OR 97462
503-459-5038

Demay and Jim Pringle are collectors. She collects dolls. He collects stamps. They both collect antiques. And they like to share them with people. So in 1983 they bought a two-story Queen Anne Victorian on a hill in Oakland that was in need of much loving restoration (Jim does woodwork; Demay sews, wallpapers and decorates). In about a year, they had redone the house with two guestrooms and were open for business as Oakland's and Douglas County's first B&B.

Another Pringle House recipe:
Sunrise Creme Caramel, page 148

Grandma Jenny's Norwegian Brown Cake

Ingredients:

    3-1/2 cups sugar
    4 cups water
    1 pound raisins
    2 cups cold water
    3/4 cup shortening
    2 tablespoons baking soda
    1 teaspoon salt
    2 teaspoons cloves
    1 teaspoon cinnamon (or more to taste)
    7 cups flour
    1 cup nuts, chopped

> Mix sugar and 4 cups water in a large saucepan or stockpot.
> Add raisins and boil until raisins have plumped, about 10 minutes.
> Remove from heat. Stir in 2 cups cold water, shortening, soda and spices. Mix well.
> Mix in flour, then add nuts.
> Pour batter into three greased bread loaf pans.
> Bake in a preheated oven at 375 degrees for 1 hour.

Makes 3 loaves

from **Home by the Sea**
2388 East Sunlight Beach Road
Clinton, WA 98236
206-221-2964

"My grandmother, Jenny Lauritz, brought this recipe from Tromsa, Norway, in 1914," said Innkeeper Sharon Fritts Drew, who remembers it being served at Christmas time. When her mother handed the recipe down to her in 1956, "My mother said, 'A sifter of flour, a pan of water, a pound of raisins, some soda, cinnamon and cloves.' We worked out these measurements." The recipe is now enjoyed by the fifth generation.

It is also enjoyed by holiday guests at Home by the Sea, which has two guest suites overlooking Useless Bay from Whidbey Island. Like the recipe, the B&B is shared by the family, with Sharon and her mother, Helen, operating it themselves. They also have private guest cottages available.

Other Home by the Sea recipes:
Sharon's Beachside Banana Bread, page 63
Pacific Northwest Breakfast Eggs, page 101
Pears Extraordinaire, page 147

Walnut Frosties

Ingredients:

1 cup plus 2 tablespoons flour
2 tablespoons powdered sugar
1/2 cup butter
1 cup brown sugar, packed
1/2 teaspoon baking soda
2 eggs, beaten
1 cup walnuts, coarsely chopped

Frosting:
2 tablespoons butter, softened
1-1/2 teaspoons orange
    juice, freshly squeezed
1-1/4 cups powdered sugar

> Combine 1 cup flour, powdered sugar and butter in a food processor until the mixture resembles coarse meal. Do not overprocess.
> Pat firmly into an ungreased 9 x 9 x 2-inch baking pan.
> Bake in a preheated oven at 350 degrees for 10 minutes. Remove and cool 5 minutes.
> Meanwhile, combine 2 tablespoons flour, brown sugar, soda and eggs. Fold in walnuts.
> Pour walnut mixture over crust. Return to oven to bake an additional 25 minutes at 350 degrees.
> For Frosting: Beat all ingredients until light and fluffy. Spread over cooled cookies. Cut into small squares.

Makes 18 cookies

from **The Morical House**
668 North Main Street
Ashland, OR 97520
503-482-2254

"During the holidays, we like to have a variety of cookies set out on the buffet in the dining room for our guests," said Innkeeper Pat Dahl. "I tried this recipe the first Christmas we were married almost three decades ago and have used it every year since then." The cookies keep well when stored in an airtight container, she reports.

The holidays are something special in this 1880s Ashland home. Pat and Pete decorate inside and out with garlands, "fairy lights," teddy bears and a 9-1/2-foot tree in the parlor. Even the weather vane, a leaping deer, sports a wreath around his neck.

All year, the restored home is decorated with period furniture and Dahls' family heirlooms. Pat and Pete became innkeepers in 1988 at the five-guestroom inn.

Other Morical House recipes:
Pina Colada Smoothies, page 22
Celebration Eggs, page 90

"Life is uncertain. Eat dessert first," reads a popular t-shirt. Well, these innkeepers may not serve dessert *first*, but they do serve it after breakfast, the first meal of the day. Why should breakfast be the one meal that gets gypped? A number of sensible innkeepers have become trend setters and incorporated dessert as a tradition at their B&B. Only one of the seven dessert recipes here includes chocolate, so Dessert for Breakfast so far seems to be a lighter fare, often incorporating fruit. And speaking of fruit, feel free to use all the recipes from the Fruits chapter as Dessert for Breakfast.

Dessert for Breakfast

Apple-Oatmeal Crumble

Ingredients:

2 or 3 tablespoons butter, melted
1/4 cup brown sugar, packed
1/4 cup quick-cooking oats
2 tablespoons flour
1/2 teaspoon cinnamon
1 or 2 teaspoons water
2 or 3 medium-size apples, peeled and sliced
2 tablespoons walnuts, chopped, optional
2 tablespoons raisins, optional

Also:

Vanilla yogurt

> In a bowl, mix butter, sugar, oats, flour and cinnamon.
> Stir in a teaspoon or two of water. Set aside.
> Place apple slices in a small pie plate or other microwave-safe bowl.
> Sprinkle with nuts and raisins and then with oat mixture.
> Microwave, uncovered, on "high" for about 2 minutes.
> Check and turn. Two more minutes may be needed to cook the apples.
> Serve hot with dollops of yogurt.
> To bake conventionally: Bake in a pie plate at 350 degrees for 20-30 minutes, until apples are tender.

Makes 4 servings

from **The White Swan Guest House**
1388 Moore Road
Mount Vernon, WA 98273
206-445-6805

"This Apple-Oatmeal Crumble is too good to pass up," said Innkeeper Peter Goldfarb, who serves it as dessert for breakfast. "I vary quantities as I make it, so this is just one way to prepare it. It is very popular in the fall and I get to use some of the many apples I get from my four different apple trees." The apple trees are part of an impressive garden, but Peter admits "the truth is, I just stick everything in the very fertile soil at random and it grows." Historic photos of this 1898 Queen Anne farmhouse in the LaConner/Skagit River Valley show gardens and trellises taking advantage of every inch of space in the yard, right up to the house.

Other White Swan Guest House recipes:
Strawberry Bread, page 65
Maple Cream Cheese, page 71
Salmon Spread, page 73
Cherry Scones, page 132

Applesauce Bread Pudding

Ingredients:
8 slices raisin bread or "Innkeeper's Choice"-brand fruit and nut bread
1/2 cup butter, softened
1 cup applesauce (homemade preferred)
2 teaspoons cinnamon
1 teaspoon nutmeg
1/2 cup brown or granulated sugar
1/2 cup raisins
3 cups milk
4 eggs
1-1/2 teaspoons vanilla extract

Also:
Cream, either light or whipped

> Spread bread with butter and saute on both sides until lightly toasted.
> Cut slices into quarters. Fit into a buttered 9 x 13-inch baking dish.
> Spread applesauce on top. Mix the spices with the sugar and sprinkle on top. Then spread the raisins on top of the sugar-spice mix.
> In a separate bowl, blend milk, eggs and vanilla.
> Pour milk mixture over other ingredients in baking dish.
> Bake in preheated oven at 350 degrees for 30-35 minutes. The pudding should be puffed and nicely browned.
> Serve warm with light or whipped cream.

Makes 6 servings

from **Turtleback Farm Inn**
Crow Valley Road
Route 1, Box 650
Orcas Island, WA 98245
206-376-4914

"This recipe was created in the kitchen at Turtleback Farm Inn to be used with Continental Bakery's brand new line of breads called 'Innkeeper's Choice,' " said Innkeeper Susan Fletcher. "This line of bread is now being test-marketed in selected parts of the country." The bread pudding makes a grand finalé to a fine breakfast at the farmhouse inn. Guests awaken refreshed and with a ravenous appetite from fresh island air and the peaceful pastoral setting on 80 inland acres overlooked by Turtleback Mountain.

Other Turtleback Farm Inn recipes:
Sesame Corn Muffins, page 48
Souffle Roll, page 104
Cornmeal Waffles, page 121

Blackberry Cobbler

Ingredients:

2 tablespoons cornstarch
2 tablespoons lemon juice
1 tablespoon sugar
1/4 cup water
4 cups fresh blackberries

Also:

Ice cream or whipped cream

Topping:
1 cup flour
1 cup sugar
1 teaspoon baking powder
1 egg
1/2 teaspoon salt
1 tablespoon butter, melted

> In a saucepan, combine cornstarch, lemon juice, sugar and water. Cook over low heat, stirring until thick.
> Fold in berries until coated.
> Pour into a greased 1-1/2-quart casserole or 6 ramekins or individual casserole dishes.
> For Topping: Combine all ingredients, except butter, stirring until mixture is crumbly.
> Sprinkle crumbly mixture over the berries. Drizzle melted butter on top.
> Bake in a preheated oven at 375 degrees for 25 minutes.
> Serve hot. May be topped with vanilla or cinnamon ice cream or whipped cream.

Makes 6 servings

from **Westwinds B&B**
4909-H Hannah Highlands Road
Friday Harbor, WA 98250
206-378-5283

"I combined two recipes, one from a friend's mother for the cobbler topping and one I made up for the berry mixture," said Innkeeper Christine Durbin, who serves this as dessert after a full breakfast. "The blackberries are picked by me from the hundreds of wild blackberry plants surrounding our wilderness spot. They are in season July through September." Sometimes guests enjoy picking a few themselves. Also on the property is a large pond that regularly hosts eagles, ducks and sometimes trumpeter swans, as well as providing drinking water for deer.

Christine and Gayle Rollins opened one suite in their contemporary home in 1988, welcoming guests to the base of Mt. Dallas on San Juan Island. Guests are treated to water and mountain views from nearly every window in the house. In the winter, guests often sit by the fire to watch a magnificent sunset or storm roll past out over the water. Summer guests enjoy riding bikes on San Juan Island's back roads and exploring historic and state parks, or beachcombing and watching for Orca whales.

Another Westwinds B&B recipe:
Singing Hinnies (Currant Scones), page 49

Chocolate Sauerkraut Cake

Ingredients:
   2/3 cup butter, softened
   1-1/2 cups sugar
   3 eggs
   1 teaspoon vanilla extract
   2-1/2 cups flour
   1 teaspoon baking soda
   1 cup water
   3 ounces (3 squares) unsweetened baking chocolate, melted
   2/3 cup sauerkraut, rinsed and drained

Also:
   Whipped cream, sweetened

> Cream butter and sugar. Mix in eggs and vanilla.
> Sift in flour and soda.
> Mix in water, chocolate and sauerkraut.
> Grease and flour a 9 x 13-inch baking pan, cupcake tins or two round layer cake pans. Pour in batter.
> Bake in a preheated oven at 350 degrees for 30 minutes for a 9 x 13-inch pan (20 minutes for cupcakes; 25 minutes for two round layer cake pans).
> "Frost" with whipped cream.

Makes 12-18 servings

from **The Ward House B&B**
516 Redwood Street
P.O. Box 86
Brookings, OR 97415
503-469-5557

"This cake is super-light, a great conversation piece because of the 'secret' ingredient (the sauerkraut), and a favorite with everyone who tries it," said Innkeeper Gro Lent. "We serve it for honeymooners and couples celebrating special days." She was given the dessert recipe by "my European girlfriend, who is an excellent gourmet cook."

Gro and husband Sheldon Lent opened their home as a B&B in 1985. Built in 1917 by Willam Ward, president of the Brookings Lumber Mill, the house overlooks downtown Brookings. The Pacific Ocean is only a few blocks away.

Other Ward House recipes:
Any Time Herbal Tea, page 18
Norwegian Waffles, page 123

Peach Pandowdy

Ingredients:

6 cups fresh peaches (or apples), peeled and sliced
3 cups sugar
1-1/2 cups flour
1-1/2 teaspoon baking powder
1/2 teaspoons salt
3/4 teaspoon cinnamon
1-1/2 cups milk
3/4 teaspoon vanilla extract
3/4 cup unsalted butter

Also:

Heavy or whipped cream

> In a large bowl, mix fruit and 1-1/2 cups sugar.
> In a separate bowl, sift remaining sugar, flour, baking powder, salt and cinnamon. Add the milk and vanilla and mix.
> Melt butter in a 9 x 13-inch baking dish.
> Stir batter into the butter.
> Spoon all the fruit on top.
> Bake in a preheated oven at 350 degrees for 35 minutes, then raise the temperature to 400 degrees and continue baking until the Pandowdy is golden around the edges.
> Serve warm with heavy cream or whipped cream.

Makes 8-10 servings

from **The Cowslip's Belle**
159 North Main Street
Ashland, OR 97520
503-488-2901

Innkeepers Carmen and Jon Reinhardt serve this often as a finale to breakfast before summer guests walk the three blocks to the Oregon Shakespeare Festival. It might be accompanied by brioche, crustless spinach quiche and a strawberry smoothie.

Reinhardts named their B&B for the cowslip flower, and the Cowslip's Belle was found in passages of "A Mid-Summer Night's Dream" and "The Tempest," among the plays performed at the summer Oregon Shakespearean Festival in Ashland. After researching various areas of the U.S. to which to move after living in the San Francisco Bay area for 21 years, Reinhardts settled on Ashland and opened their B&B in this 1913 Craftsman bungalow and carriage house. The four guestrooms have Elizabethian names of flowers.

Another Cowslip's Belle recipe:
Chocolate Mousse Truffles, page 154

Pears Extraordinaire

Ingredients:
>1 fresh pear
>1 tablespoon cream cheese, softened
>1 teaspoon honey
>1/4 teaspoon vanilla extract ("I prefer to use Mexican vanilla")

Also:
>Apple juice or favorite liqueur
>Fresh berries
>Mint leaves

> Peel pear if the skin is coarse. Slice the pear in half and core.
> In a microwave-safe dish, place pear cut side down. Add a few drops water, apple juice or favorite liqueur.
> Cover and microwave on medium for 5 minutes to poach the pear, until the pear is soft and hot but not mushy.
> In a separate bowl, mix the cream cheese, honey and vanilla.
> Flip the pear over so cut side is up. Place half of the cream cheese mixture in the center of each pear half. Garnish with fresh berries and mint.

Makes 2 servings

from **Home by the Sea**
2388 East Sunlight Beach Road
Clinton, WA 98236
206-221-2964

"Our guests rave about this and often guess the ingredients, and they are amazed to find the simplicity," said Innkeeper Sharon Fritts Drew. She credits her sister, Jean Fritts Alexander, with creating the recipe.

"This is a family-run business," she says of her B&B, in which her sister and her mother, Helen, also participate. The Whidbey Island home is literally by the sea, on Useless Bay, and guests dine inside or on the patio overlooking the driftwood-strewn beach. Because the home faces southeast, lots of good water traffic can be seen from here.

Other Home by the Sea recipes:
Sharon's Beachside Banana Bread, page 63
Pacific Northwest Breakfast Eggs, page 101
Grandma Jenny's Norwegian Brown Cake, page 138

Sunrise Creme Caramel

Ingredients:

    1/2 cup sugar
    4 eggs
    2 cups milk
    1 teaspoon vanilla extract
    1/4 teaspoon salt

Also:

    Mandarin orange segments or strawberries, sliced
    Whipped cream

> In a small pan over medium heat, heat 1/4 cup sugar, stirring constantly until the sugar has melted and is light caramel in color.
> Immediately pour into six custard cups.
> In a large bowl, beat eggs and remaining 1/4 cup sugar well.
> Beat in milk, vanilla and salt until well-mixed.
> Pour egg mixture over caramel in custard cups.
> Place cups in a 9 x 13-inch baking pan. Fill the pan with hot water to come 1/3-way up the sides of the cups.
> Bake in a preheated oven at 325 degrees for 50-55 minutes, until a knife inserted in the center comes out clean.
> Remove cups from pan. Let cool, then cover with foil and refrigerate until chilled, about 90 minutes.
> To remove from cups, insert a knife around the edges. Carefully turn cup over on a serving plate to allow the liquid caramel to flow over the custard.
> Garnish with mandarin orange segments to form a sunburst design, or use sliced strawberries. Add a dollop of whipped cream.

Makes 6 servings

from **The Pringle House B&B**
Locust at 7th Streets
P.O. Box 578
Oakland, OR 97462
503-459-5038

"Sensational!" is the response Innkeeper Demay Pringle gets when she serves this dessert for breakfast in the formal dining room of this National Register of Historic Places home. Guests enjoy breakfast seated in pressback chairs, with lace tablecloth and curtains, amid collections of steins, plates and antiques. Demay and Jim, a retired music teacher, completely renovated this home, built by a local merchant to overlook downtown. Pringles wanted to "retire" into the B&B business, and they opened two guestrooms in 1984.

Another Pringle House recipe:
Eggnog French Toast Almondine, page 137

A "bottomless" cookie jar. Chocolate Mousse Truffles by the bedside. Appetizers served at a social hour or a dish of cobbler or crisp with a glass of lemonade on the porch. All are symbols of hospitality, and these innkeepers know that food can help a guest feel at home. The following 14 recipes were not served for breakfast or didn't fit well into another category. But all definitely are favorite recipes that innkeepers make over and over again, often by request of repeat visitors. Perhaps they will make your list of frequent favorite recipes, as well!

Other Favorites

Bombay House Granola

Ingredients:

6 cups quick oats
1/2 cup brown sugar, packed
3/4 cup wheat germ
1/2 cup oat bran
1/2 cup flaked coconut
1/2 cup sunflower seeds
1/2 cup sesame seeds
3/4 cup nuts, chopped
1/2 cup pine nuts
1/2 cup non-fat dry milk
1/2 cup honey
1/2 cup vegetable oil
1/4 cup water
1 tablespoon vanilla extract
1 cup golden raisins or currants
1 cup dried fruit, chopped (optional)

> Combine oats, brown sugar, wheat germ, oat bran, coconut, seeds, nuts and dry milk. Turn into two shallow baking pans.
> In a covered jar, shake honey, oil, water and vanilla until mixed.
> Pour half of liquid mixture over each panful of granola. Stir until all dry particles are moistened.
> Bake in a preheated oven at 300 degrees for 20-30 minutes or just until lightly toasted, stirring at least twice during baking.
> Add raisins and dried fruit and bake 5 minutes more.
> Stir occasionally while cooling. Store in tightly-sealed containers. "It freezes well!"

Makes about 3 quarts

from **The Bombay House B&B**
8490 Beck Road NE
Bainbridge Island, WA 98110
206-842-3926

Combined with fresh Bainbridge Island raspberries or other fruit, this gives Bunny Cameron and Roger Kanchuck's guests energy for a long day of beachcombing, clam digging, fishing, golfing or other island pursuits.

Other Bombay House recipes:
Morning Raspberry Cake, page 28
English Muffin Bread, page 59
Citrus Fruit Dip, page 81

Cedarym Oats

Ingredients:

8 cups old-fashioned oats
3/4 cup dark brown sugar, packed
1-1/2 cups almonds, sliced
1-1/2 cups wheat germ
1 cup oat bran
1-1/2 cups raw sunflower seeds
1-1/2 cups safflower oil
3/4 cup honey
2 teaspoons vanilla extract
1 teaspoon apple pie spice
2 cups currants, dried (or raisins or dates)

> In a very large bowl, combine oats, brown sugar, almonds, wheat germ, oat bran and seeds.
> In a small sauce pan, combine oil, honey, vanilla and spice. Heat only until bubbles form;
do not boil.
> Pour liquid mixture over dry ingredients and mix until dry ingredients are well-coated.
> Spread in a large baking pan that has been sprayed with a non-stick spray.
> Bake in a preheated oven at 325 degrees, stirring frequently, until nicely browned,
45-60 minutes.
> Remove from oven and stir in currants. Stir frequently while cooling.
> Store in the freezer in an airtight container.

Makes 14 cups

from **Cedarym**
1011 240th Avenue NE
Redmond, WA 98053
206-868-4159

"The recipe has evolved over several years. It was initially made as Christmas gifts," said Innkeeper Mary Ellen Brown. The name was changed from "Mom's Granola," and coconut was removed to lower cholesterol.

Mary Ellen and Walt have created an authentic colonial B&B with modern comforts. Each piece of furniture is correct for the period, plus special features, like openings above the mantle of the walk-in hearth (the gunpowder would have been stored there to keep it dry). Browns have two guestrooms and say their guests often are area residents who want to drive only a short time but find themselves decades away in a time gone by.

Other Cedarym recipes:
Festive Marmalade, page 70
Surprise French Toast, page 111
Christmas Stollen, page 134

Cheese Olive Appetizers

Ingredients:

1/2 pound sharp cheddar cheese, grated
1/2 cup butter, softened
Dash of Worchestershire sauce
1 cup flour
1/2 teaspoon salt
7-ounce or smaller jar of large pimento-stuffed green olives, drained

> In a medium bowl, blend shredded cheese and butter with an electric mixer.
> Beat in Worchestershire sauce.
> Then beat in flour and salt.
> Wrap each olive in a teaspoonful of dough. Roll each in the palm of hands to make a ball.
> Spread the balls in a pan to freeze or refrigerate. (If freezing, remove frozen balls from pan and store in freezer bags until use.)
> Place frozen or refrigerated cheese balls on an ungreased cookie sheet.
> Bake in a preheated oven at 425 degrees for 12 minutes. Serve hot.

Makes about 2 dozen

from **The Victorian B&B**
602 North Main Street
Coupeville, WA 98239
206-678-5305

Innkeeper Dolores Fresh may serve this to guests in the afternoon or for an evening snack. She's enjoyed serving it at parties, and says the frozen cheese balls are handy to keep in the freezer until ready to bake.

Dolores purchased this large Coupeville home in 1988, offering two guest-rooms and a private cottage to guests exploring Whidbey Island. Coupeville is home to one of the nation's largest historic preserves, Ebey's Landing National Historic Preserve, created by Congress in 1980. Front Street, along the waterfront, has restored shops and businesses in Victorian-era buildings. Many of the town's vintage homes also have been restored.

The Victorian home was built in 1889 by Bertha and Jacob Jenne, who used their savings from farming to build the house, and bought a downtown hotel two years later. Five years after Jacob's death in 1908, Bertha remarried. Her husband, Dr. Thomas White, was a dentist who moved his office to this property, in back of the house. Today his office is a private guest cottage.

Another Victorian B&B recipe:
Cinnamon Pecans, page 135

Chip 'n Dale Chocolate Chip Cookies

Ingredients:

6 ounces (3/4 cup plus 2 tablespoons) brown sugar, unpacked
6 ounces (3/4 cup plus 2 tablespoons) sugar
8 ounces (1 cup) and 1 tablespoon margarine, at room temperature
2 large eggs
1 teaspoon vanilla extract
17 ounces (3-1/2 cups plus 4 tablespoons) unbleached flour
1 teaspoon baking soda
1 teaspoon salt
12-ounce package miniature semi-sweet chocolate chips

> In a large bowl, cream sugars and margarine.
> Break eggs into a measuring cup. If necessary, add water to make 1/2 cup. Then add eggs and vanilla to sugar mixture. Beat until smooth.
> Blend in dry ingredients. Dough will be very stiff.
> Mix in chocolate chips by hand.
> Drop onto a double or thermal cookie sheet "in small globs — half golfball size."
> Bake in a preheated oven at 350 degrees, 12 minutes for chewy cookie, 14-15 for crispy.

Makes about 55 cookies

from **Eagles Nest Inn**
3236 East Saratoga Road
Langley, WA 98260
206-321-5331

Innkeeper Dale Bowman has perfected his recipe over the years, testing on co-workers in the Navy, and eventually selling the cookies for two years at work. They are now always on hand in the "bottomless" cookie jar.

Dale has several notes: "The reasons for weighing the sugar and flour is to obtain better consistency from batch to batch." He made his extra-thick cookie sheet from sheet aluminum, but says new "double" or thermal sheets work as well. Margarine makes a chewier cookie ("Surprisingly, most testers — 90 percent — liked the version using margarine instead of butter"). The thick dough keeps the cookie from going flat, and the well-tested flour-sugar ratio means this cookie is not too sweet.

Dale and Nancy opened three rooms in their new B&B in 1987. An outdoor whirlpool tub helps soak away guests' guilt if they over-indulge in cookies.

Other Eagles Nest Inn recipes:
Raspberry Muffins, page 46
Ricotta Cheese Pancakes, page 120

Chocolate Mousse Truffles

Ingredients:

12 ounces semi-sweet chocolate, broken into small pieces
1/4 cup unsalted butter, quartered
3/4 cup heavy cream
1 egg white, beaten until stiff

Chocolate Coating:
8 ounces semi-sweet chocolate

> For the Ganache (truffle center): Melt chocolate and butter (microwave at intervals of 30-seconds to 1-minute), stirring until smooth.
> Scald cream. Strain.
> Mix cream and melted chocolate completely.
> Gradually stir in egg white. Mixture should be frothy.
> Cover and refrigerate in a large glass plan until ganache is firm.
> Line a baking sheet with waxed paper. Using a melon baller, spoon 1-inch mounds onto the paper. Refrigerate again until firm.
> Rinse hands with cold water and dry. Rub palms with powdered sugar. Roll each mound into a smooth ball and refrigerate again.
> For Coating: Melt 8 ounces chocolate pieces to 105 degrees, stirring occasionally.
> Remove from heat and cool to 89 degrees.
> Dip each ball quickly. Shake off excess chocolate.
> Place truffles on waxed paper. Refrigerate again for 45 minutes.
> Place truffles in paper candy cups and then in an airtight container. Truffles may be refrigerated for up to two weeks (but who can wait that long?).

Makes 22-24 truffles

from **The Cowslip's Belle**
159 North Main Street
Ashland, OR 97520
503-488-2901

"We developed this recipe ourselves," said Innkeeper Carmen Reinhardt, after much personal truffle tasting. A truffle appears on pillows before bed. "It was such a hit we started making other special chocolate desserts and now we have our chocolate creations in several of the restaurants in town."

Carmen and Jon opened this four-guestroom B&B in 1985. They bought a 1913 Craftsman bungalow with a carriage house, in which two guestrooms have been opened. "Jon has done almost all of the restoration himself with the help of a wonderful assistant — me!" Carmen notes. They have filled their home with antiques from the 1890s through 1920s eras, and the rooms have handmade quilts and members of the teddy bear collection.

Another Cowslip's Belle recipe:
Peach Pandowdy, page 146

Good and Good-for-You Yummie Cookies

Ingredients:

1 cup butter, melted
1-1/2 cups brown sugar, packed
2 eggs
2 teaspoons vanilla extract
1 cup raisins
1-1/2 cups whole wheat flour
1 teaspoon baking powder
1 teaspoon salt
2 cups old-fashioned rolled or quick oats
1 cup coconut
3/4 cup sunflower seeds

> In a large bowl, mix butter and brown sugar.
> Mix in eggs and vanilla. Then stir in raisins.
> In a separate bowl, mix flour, baking powder and salt. Mix into egg mixture.
> Stir in oats, coconut and seeds.
> Drop spoonfulls onto greased baking sheets.
> Bake in a preheated oven at 350 degrees for 10 minutes.

Makes 3 dozen cookies

from **Marit's B&B**
6208 Palatine Avenue N.
Seattle, WA 98103
206-782-7900

These cookies may go into a lunch or snack box for guests heading for a day of sightseeing or picnicking at the Woodland Park Zoo or Green Lake, within walking distance of Marit and Carl Nelson's home. Marit also tucks some in for those heading home, and Carl makes sure to get his fair share.

In 1982, after 25 years of cooking for five children and three years of college, Marit discovered that running her own small business in this metropolitan area was just her ticket. She and Carl have opened two guestrooms and offer European hospitality, the kind Marit learned first hand growing up in Norway.

Other Marit's B&B recipes:
Golden Raisin Scones, page 41
Norwegian Pancakes with Lingonberry Cream, page 119

Grandma Jessie Bell's Scotch Shortbread

Ingredients:

    1 pound butter, softened
    1 cup "superfine" sugar
    3 cups flour
    1 cup white rice flour

Also:

    Powdered sugar

> Work the butter with an electric mixer until it is smooth and creamy. Then gradually work in the sugar, creaming thoroughly.
> Sift in the flours a little at a time, mixing in quickly.
> Lightly dust two sheets of waxed paper with powdered sugar. Roll out one-third of the dough between the two sheets until it is 1/2 to 3/4-inch thick.
> Cut dough with a deep cookie cutter ("I use one with fluted edges that measures 1-5/6-inch on the cutting edge.")
> Place cookies on an ungreased cookie sheet. Prick several times with a fine-tined fork all the way through.
> Bake in a preheated oven at 325 degrees for 5 minutes, then at 300 degrees for 15-20 minutes.

Makes 6 dozen small cookies

from **Mildred's B&B**
1201 15th Avenue E.
Seattle, WA 98112
206-325-6072

"Baked shortbread should be light in color, not browned at all — just a trifle tan on the bottom," warns Innkeeper Mildred Sarver. She watches the cookies carefully during the last few minutes of cooking. And then she watches guests devour them. "I always keep these on hand to serve to guests when they first arrive or in the evening for a snack with tea or coffee."

One of Mildred's fondest memories is of opening the Christmas package from her grandmother, which always contained a box of homemade shortbread. The recipe was passed down to Mildred's mother, Grandma Jessie Bell, who emigrated from Scotland to Canada at age 25, and then it was passed down to Mildred. Mildred opened her family home as a three-guestroom B&B on Capitol Hill in 1982.

Other Mildred's B&B recipes:
Bran Muffins with Sesame Seed, page 37
No-Crust Smoked Salmon Quiche, page 100

Greek Ground Lamb Appetizers

Ingredients:

2 pounds lean ground lamb
2 eggs, beaten
2/3 cup cracker crumbs
2/3 cup soy sauce
4 tablespoons water
1/8 teaspoon each:
    ginger, garlic powder, cumin
1/2 cup walnuts or pine nuts

Dip:
    1/2 cup honey
    1/2 cup prepared mustard

> Mix all ingredients thoroughly (clean hands work best).
> Shape into 1-inch balls and place on a jelly roll sheet or baking pan.
> Bake in a preheated oven at 300 degrees for 35-40 minutes. (The cooked appetizers can be frozen and reheated in a microwave.)
> Serve with a honey/mustard dip, if desired.

Makes 50-60 meatballs

from **Sonka's Sheep Station Inn**
901 NW Chadwick Lane
Myrtle Creek, OR 97457
503-863-5168

Innkeeper Evelyn Sonka's recipe, served as appetizers for B&B dinner guests, was a prize winner at a local Lamb Cook-off Contest. "Many of our guests enjoy the opportunity to taste lamb for the first time," she said.

Evelyn, Louis and son Joe market lambs from 700 commercial ewes on their 300-acre ranch. Ranching is nothing new to them: before moving to the Oregon ranch, they raised sheep and apples in the Mother Lode foothills of California. After a farm tour in New Zealand, they decided to try offering a farmstay in their comfortable Oregon home. Since then, Evelyn has interested other area farms in opening as B&Bs, and she's found many guests love the opportunity to help with chores or herding.

Douglas County, where the ranch is located, is the largest sheep producing county in Oregon. Sonka's entire home is "sheepish," with sheep motif on kitchen wallpaper, bathroom linens, original art and flannel sheets.

Another Sonka's Sheep Station Inn recipe:
Fancy Egg Scramble, page 98

High Energy Fruit Balls

Ingredients:

    1 cup dried apricots, black mission figs, dates or a mixture
    1/2 cup walnuts
    1/2 cup hulled sesame seeds
    1/2 cup sunflower seeds
    1/2 cup pumpkin seeds
    2 tablespoons carob powder
    1/2 cup unsweetened coconut

> In a bowl, cover dried fruit with boiling water and soak overnight. In the morning, drain the fruit (reserve the liquid).
> Chop the soaked fruit — a food processor works well.
> In a coffee grinder, grind the walnuts and seeds.
> Add seeds and nuts to fruit in the food processor and mix thoroughly. Add a little of the reserved liquid, if necessary to mix well.
> Add carob powder and blend again.
> Spoon out mixture and roll into balls.
> Roll each ball in coconut. Place in truffle or paper candy cups. "These freeze well."

Makes 12-18 servings

from **Umpqua House of Oregon**
7338 Oak Hill Road
Roseburg, OR 97470
503-459-4700

Innkeeper Rhoda Mozorosky invented this recipe to serve to guests as a snack, or if they request a packed lunch for fishing or hiking. As a nutritional counselor, Rhoda often experiments with recipes to make them healthful. Guests most likely are treated to fresh fruit, produce and eggs from her organic garden, and she enjoys preparing fresh food from scratch.

Rhoda and Allen moved into this house in July 1986 and "building, remodeling and repairing has kept him very busy," Rhoda says of her husband. They moved to these 6.5 acres with a view of the Umpqua Valley specifically to open a two-guestroom B&B.

Other Umpqua House recipes:
Fruit Smoothie, page 19
Cranberry Crisp Coffeecake, page 27
Pumpkin Muffins, page 45

Inn at Swifts Bay Potatoes

Ingredients:

4 to 6 baked potatoes, thoroughly chilled
1/2 to 1 pound bacon, chopped (low-salt preferred)
1 large yellow onion, chopped
1 teaspoon rough-ground black pepper
1/2 cup brown sugar, packed
1 teaspoon seasoned salt (Lawry's preferred)
1 to 2 teaspoons white vinegar
3 to 5 dashes hot pepper sauce

Also:

Paprika
Fresh parsley, chopped

> Peel baked potatoes and cut into one-inch chunks.
> Cook bacon until almost crisp. Add onion and saute until it is translucent.
> Add black pepper, brown sugar and seasoned salt. Cook over medium heat until a syrup starts to form.
> Add vinegar and hot pepper sauce. Cook and stir briefly.
> Add potatoes and stir to coat.
> Place mixture in top of a double boiler. Cook for 30-45 minutes, stirring occasionally to equalize heat. Potatoes are done when the flavors have melded. "You will see and taste the difference as they cook." (This dish may be reheated.)
> Serve garnished with paprika and fresh parsley.

Makes 8-10 servings

from **The Inn at Swifts Bay**
Port Stanley Road
Route 2, Box 3402
Lopez Island, WA 98261
206-468-3636

Innkeeper Chris Brandmeir created this recipe when he was a brunch chef in Napa, Calif. "We continue to use it here at the inn as a winter accompaniment. Amounts may be easily adjusted for taste. The sugar/vinegar gives a sweet and sour flavor with pungent pepper." Breakfasts are something special here because of the restaurant expertise of Chris and partner Robert Herrmann. Their Tudor-style inn, situated in a country setting, is two miles from the ferry landing, and withing walking or biking distance of two parks and Lopez Village.

Other Inn at Swifts Bay recipes:
Asparagus Herb Cheese Omelettes, page 88
Eggs Dungeness, page 95

Our Favorite Oatmeal-Raisin Cookie

Ingredients:

- 1 cup butter or margarine, softened
- 3/4 cup sugar
- 1/2 teaspoon salt
- 1 teaspoon baking soda
- 1/4 teaspoon nutmeg
- 1 teaspoon vanilla extract
- 2 eggs
- 1 tablespoon lemon juice
- 1 cup raisins
- 1/2 cup nuts, optional
- 1-1/2 cups whole wheat pastry flour
- 3 cups old-fashioned rolled or quick oats

> Cream butter and sugar.
> Mix in salt, soda, nutmeg and vanilla.
> Beat in eggs and lemon juice, then stir in raisins and nuts.
> In a separate bowl, mix flour and oats. Gradually blend it into the egg mixture.
> Shape into 1-inch balls and place two inches apart on a greased cookie sheet.
> Bake in a preheated oven at 350 degrees for 12-15 minutes.

Makes 6 dozen cookies

from **Spring Creek Llama Ranch**
14700 NE Spring Creek Lane
Newberg, OR 97132
503-538-5717

"My grandmother used to make these cookies. Then my mother passed the recipe to me," said Innkeeper Melinda Van Bossuyt. "Over the years, I have gradually changed the recipe to include wholegrain flour and much less sugar and salt. Our guests often join us for a late afternoon or evening snack. These cookies are enjoyed with tea or a glass of milk."

In addition to the cookies, guests sometimes want to take home one of the "boys" on the ranch — Melinda and Dave's term for their llamas. The gentle animals even accompany Melinda on nursing home visits. "The llamas go right inside and walk up to the beds and wheelchairs to give kisses and let folks pet their necks."

Other Spring Creek Llama Ranch recipes:
Melinda's Whole Wheat Blueberry Muffins, page 43
Naturally Sweet Fruit Syrup, page 72
Melinda's Famous Wholegrain Waffles, page 122

Quick Cobbler

Ingredients:
>   1/2 cup butter
>   1 cup flour
>   1 tablespoon baking powder
>   1 cup plus 2 tablespoons sugar
>   3/4 cup milk
>   2 cups fresh apples or peaches, peeled and sliced, or berries (or 1 16-ounce can fruit)

Also:
>   Vanilla ice cream or heavy cream

> Melt the butter in a 13 x 9 x 2-inch baking dish.
> In a separate bowl, mix flour, baking powder and 1 cup sugar well with the milk.
> Pour flour mixture over the butter. Top with fruit.
> Sprinkle with 2 tablespoons sugar. (Optional: add 1/2 teaspoon cinnamon, nutmeg or ginger to sugar, depending on the type of fruit used.)
> Bake in a preheated oven at 350 degrees for 30 minutes, until well-browned.
> Serve warm with ice cream or in deep bowls with heavy cream.

Makes 8 servings

from **Ahlf House B&B**
762 NW 6th Street
Grants Pass, OR 97526
503-474-1374

This recipe "smells absolutely wonderful when baking," said Innkeeper Betty Buskirk. "We serve it with ice cream to our guests at our Victorian evening, while guests are being entertained with piano music." "Victorian evening" is held every night at 8 in the front parlor with the hosts playing the piano and visiting with guests.

The cobbler also is a fitting dessert for breakfast. Breakfast in this large Queen Anne mansion is in the formal dining room. Blue-and-white is a decorative theme, with a blue-and-white Christmas plate collection on the wall and a beautiful, large blue-and-white Oriental rug underfoot.

Betty, who worked in libraries, and Rosemary Althaus, a retired surgical nurse, became partners and opened their three-guestroom B&B in 1986.

Another Ahlf House recipe:
Fluffy Fingers French Toast, page 107

Shortbread Cookies

Ingredients:
- 1 pound butter, softened
- 1-1/4 cups sugar
- 2 egg yolks
- 4-1/2 cups flour
- 1 teaspoon vanilla extract
- 1/4 teaspoon almond extract, optional

> Using an electric beater, cream the butter and sugar until the mixture is light and fluffy.
> Beat in the egg yolks and extracts.
> Remove the beaters. Stir in the flour by hand.
> Pinch off the batter and roll into 1-inch balls.
> Place the balls on an ungreased cookie sheet and press with a cookie stamp or floured fork.
> Bake in a preheated oven at 325 degrees for 20-25 minutes, until golden brown.

Makes 4-5 dozen

from **The Willows B&B**
5025 Homesteader Road
Wilsonville, OR 97070
503-638-3722

"We like to serve these while enjoying an afternoon pause with our guests on the front lawn under our huge old willow tree," said Innkeeper Shirlee Key. "These cookies, a recipe from a Canadian friend, go well with a glass of home-pressed apple juice." These rich cookies no doubt would make any beverage go down easier.

Located just 20 minutes from Portland, Shirlee and Dave's B&B is on two hilly acres cut by a creek. Guests can sit under the willows, smell the flowers, or talk with Keys about their travels. A path from the house leads down to the creek, where trilliums are out in the early spring, followed by buttercups and then yellow and orange vine maple in the fall.

Summer guests might get to share some of Key's homegrown raspberries, and many of the breakfasts feature fresh eggs from their Bantam chickens. After moving here from Houston in 1984 to "retire," they opened the B&B in 1986. Since then, others also have found out what Shirlee Key means when she says it's "our special retirement paradise."

Another Willows B&B recipe:
Apple Dutch Babies with Cinnamon Candy Syrup, page 112

Wild Blackberry Crisp

Ingredients:

1 quart (4 cups) wild blackberries, fresh or frozen
3/4 cup sugar
1/4 cup flour

Topping:
1/2 cup butter, chilled
2/3 cup brown sugar, packed
1-1/3 cups flour

Also:

Whipped cream or vanilla ice cream

> Mix berries, sugar and flour. Place in a greased 9 x 9-inch baking dish.
> In a separate bowl, cut the topping ingredients together with a pastry blender or fork until crumbly.
> Sprinkle topping over blackberries.
> Bake in a preheated oven at 375 degrees for about 45 minutes.
> Serve warm with a scoop of ice cream or whipped cream.

Makes 6 servings

from **Miller Tree Inn**
East Division Street
P.O. Box 953
Forks, WA 98331
206-374-6806

Innkeepers Prue and Ted Miller welcome fishermen back from a day of steelhead, salmon or trout fishing with a bowl of this local treat. Forks, named for the forks of numerous rivers, has no less than six clear steelhead rivers nearby, and Prue and Ted cheerfully pack and freeze the day's catch for guests. They'll also pack lunches for day hikers and fishermen.

Millers opened six guestrooms in 1984 "after falling in love with this 1917 homestead on its three acres," Prue said. The white clapboard house was once a farm home. Prue, who worked at the local newspaper, and Ted, formerly in the logging industry, turned the six rooms on the second floor into guestrooms, catering to fishermen and those who love the Olympic Peninsula. Even teenage daughter Katie pitches in, "wielding a mean dust cloth and doing lightning bedsheet changes," her mom reported.

Breakfast here includes Prue's homemade baked goods and jam and Ted's eggs, served any style. Guests can sit in the farmhouse kitchen and chat with the hosts while breakfast is being made. Millers gladly give advice and directions on attractions, such as the Sol Duc Hot Springs, the Hoh Rain Forest, Rialto Beach, or several hiking trails and fishing holes.

Place other favorite recipes here

Place other favorite recipes here

Contents by Inn

WASHINGTON

Traveling to these B&Bs?

Need more information before heading out? Contact the state B&B associations for a listing of member inns. Contact state travel offices for maps and publications. Also, check your bookstore's regional section for B&B guides which do not charge B&Bs to be included.

Oregon

Oregon Bed & Breakfast Guild
P.O. Box 3187
Ashland, OR 97520
Write for a free brochure listing more than 50 member inns.

Oregon B&B Directory
230 Red Spur Dr.
Grants Pass, OR 98527
Send $1 and a self-addressed, stamped #10 (business) envelope for a brochure listing 116 Oregon inns.

Oregon Tourism Division
775 Summer Street NE
Salem, OR 97310
503-378-3451
1-800-547-7842 from out-of-state
1-800-543-8838 in Oregon

Washington

Washington State Bed & Breakfast Guild
2442 NW Market St.
Seattle, WA 98107
Write for a free brochure listing more than 110 member inns.

Washington State Tourism Division
101 General Administration Building
Olympia, WA 98504
206-753-5600
1-800-544-1800

Ordering Information

Order additional copies of any of the editions from your bookstore or by mail.

☛ *WAKE UP & SMELL THE COFFEE* - **Pacific Northwest** Edition features more than 130 of innkeepers' best recipes from 58 B&Bs in Washington and Oregon. The travel Information on each B&B makes this book double as a travel guide, and means it's a fun read - more than just recipes!
Cost: $11.95 plus $3.00 postage and handling = $13.95 per book

COMPLETE YOUR COLLECTION!

If you enjoyed this book, you'll love *WAKE UP & SMELL THE COFFEE - Southwest Edition* and *Lake States Edition.* And look for the *Northern New England* (ME, VT & NH) Edition coming soon!

☛ *Southwest Edition* boasts more than 170 recipes from 65 B&Bs in Texas, Arizona and New Mexico, along with the helpful cooking hints and interesting details on each inn.
Cost: $14.95 plus $3.00 postage and handling = $17.95 per book

☛ *Lake States Edition* has 203 recipes from 125 B&Bs in Michigan, Wisconsin and Michigan, with tester's comments -- the largest of the four books.
Cost: $15.95 plus $3.00 postage and handling = $18.95 per book

TO ORDER BY MAIL, send a check to Down to Earth Publications, 1032 W. Montana, St. Paul, MN 55117. Make checks payable to Down to Earth Publications. MN residents please add 7% sales tax.

Mail to: Down to Earth Publications
1032 W. Montana
St. Paul, MN 55117

Please send me:
_____ "WAKE UP & SMELL THE COFFEE - *Pacific Northwest* Edition" at $14.95 each by 4th class mail ($15.95 each sent UPS ground service)

_____ "WAKE UP & SMELL THE COFFEE - *Lake States* Edition" at $18.95 each by 4th class mail ($19.95 each sent UPS ground service)

_____ "WAKE UP & SMELL THE COFFEE - *Southwest* Edition" at $17.95 each by 4th class mail ($18.95 each sent UPS ground service)

I have enclosed $_____ for _____ book(s). Send it/them to:

Name: _____

Street: _____ Apt. No. _____

City: _____ State: _____ Zip: _____
(Please note: No P.O. Boxes for UPS delivery)

Ordering Information

Order additional copies of any of the editions from your bookstore or by mail.

☞ **WAKE UP & SMELL THE COFFEE - Pacific Northwest** Edition features more than 130 of innkeepers' best recipes from 58 B&Bs in Washington and Oregon. The travel Information on each B&B makes this book double as a travel guide, and means it's a fun read - more than just recipes!
Cost: $11.95 plus $3.00 postage and handling = $13.95 per book

COMPLETE YOUR COLLECTION!

If you enjoyed this book, you'll love *WAKE UP & SMELL THE COFFEE - Southwest Edition* and *Lake States Edition*. And look for the **Northern New England** (ME, VT & NH) Edition coming soon!

☞ *Southwest Edition* boasts more than 170 recipes from 65 B&Bs in Texas, Arizona and New Mexico, along with the helpful cooking hints and interesting details on each inn.
Cost: $14.95 plus $3.00 postage and handling = $17.95 per book

☞ *Lake States Edition* has 203 recipes from 125 B&Bs in Michigan, Wisconsin and Michigan, with tester's comments -- the largest of the four books.
Cost: $15.95 plus $3.00 postage and handling = $18.95 per book

TO ORDER BY MAIL, send a check to Down to Earth Publications, 1032 W. Montana, St. Paul, MN 55117. Make checks payable to Down to Earth Publications. MN residents please add 7% sales tax.

Mail to: Down to Earth Publications
1032 W. Montana
St. Paul, MN 55117

Please send me:
_____ "WAKE UP & SMELL THE COFFEE - *Pacific Northwest* Edition" at $14.95 each by 4th class mail ($15.95 each sent UPS ground service)

_____ "WAKE UP & SMELL THE COFFEE - *Lake States* Edition" at $18.95 each by 4th class mail ($19.95 each sent UPS ground service)

_____ "WAKE UP & SMELL THE COFFEE - *Southwest* Edition" at $17.95 each by 4th class mail ($18.95 each sent UPS ground service)

I have enclosed $_____ for _____ book(s). Send it/them to:

Name: _____

Street: _____ Apt. No. _____

City: _____ State: _____ Zip: _____
(Please note: No P.O. Boxes for UPS delivery)

About the author

Laura Zahn discovered the wonderful "Breakfast" part of "Bed & Breakfast" while traveling the backroads of Minnesota, Wisconsin and Illinois to write her "Room at the Inn/Minnesota," "Room at the Inn/Wisconsin" and "Room at the Inn/Galena Area" guidebooks to historic B&Bs and country inns.

She discovered the wonderful Pacific Northwest while living and working in Southeast Alaska as a newspaper reporter. It would be a nice place to live, but for now she visits as often as she can. The pleasure of Pacific Northwest food is one reason she keeps coming back.

In St. Paul, Minn., she is president of Down to Earth Publications, a writing, publishing and public relations firm specializing in travel. Her travelwriting has appeared in many U.S. newspapers and magazines. Zahn has worked in public relations in Minnesota and as a reporter and editor on newspapers in Alaska and Minnesota.

"Wake Up and Smell the Coffee - Pacific Northwest Edition" is her sixth book. In addition to the three "Room at the Inn" guides now in print and "Wake Up and Smell the Coffee - Upper Midwest Edition," she is co-author of "Ride Guide to the Historic Alaska Railroad."

A native of Saginaw, Michigan, she passed a written test to win the "Betty Crocker Homemaker of the Year" award in high school and says, "Now I've finally done something remotely related, besides tour the Betty Crocker kitchens." She graduated from Northern Michigan University in Marquette. She shares her St. Paul home with Jim Miller, her geologist husband, and Kirby Puckett Zahn Miller, who was proudly adopted from the Humane Society of Ramsey County on the day the Minnesota Twins won the American League pennant in 1987.